THE SEVEN AGES OF WILLIAM SHAKESPEARE

A PLAY ABOUT HIS LIFE

TO THE ACTORS.

All of the parts in this play can be played by a boy or girl, a man or a woman. In William's time all parts were played by men or boys, so I am sure he would be delighted with this direction.

I ask that whatever the sex of the player, all the roles are to be performed authentically and in costume appropriate to that time.

I intended that there be seven Shakespeare's in this play, one for each of the Acts but I will leave the number with the director with no less than three actors playing his role as he ages.

One other matter; due to the length of the play, the director should choose a place for an intermission, to let the audience rest and refresh themselves. I give my thanks to the actors who will play my words and those of the Bard.

PROLOGUE.
Read by Ben Jonson

Enter Benjamin Jonson (center stage, it is dark but a spotlight illuminates him, he, dressed in Elizabethan doublet, pantaloon and hose)

Jonson   I ask that you forgive my sad attire, for I am very old and have returned to this world to speak of my beloved friend William Shakespeare. I was drinking with William a few nights before he left this world, and in that universe of his company it was easy to forget he was a human being like you and I; easy to forget that he could fall prey to fatigue or illness, but then he did.

Filled with the grief of his loss I threw away all envy and scores unsettled; I mean to tell you he owed me nothing and I owed him all, but during our time together as a small man might, I convinced myself he owed me even if it were just his companionship.

So in his death I found myself and my spirit threw off my jealousy and competitiveness and I wrote a poetic eulogy to him and, by grief, stripped of all my faults I tried to be true.

I will give you a little of what I wrote:
I called my eulogy, "To the Memory of My Beloved, The Author, Mr. William Shakespeare, and What He Hath Left Us."

Because my own talent was so great I considered myself the proper person to write these lines,
"To draw no envy, Shakespeare, on thy name
Am I thus ample to thy book and fame;
While I confess thy writings to be such
As neither Man nor Muse can praise too much."

From this you can see modesty was not my forte, but my point is that it made it all the more difficult for me to see genius in another.But bear with me and allow me to continue?I therefore will begin: "

Soul of the Age!
The applause, delight, the wonder of our stage!
My Shakespeare, rise"

and then

"Thou art a monument without a tomb,
And art alive still, while thy book doth live,
And we have wits to read, and praise to give."

But then my triumphal oration

"To live again, to hear thy buskin tread,
And shake a stage; or, when thy socks were on,
Leave thee alone for the comparison
Of all that insolent Greece or haughty Rome
Sent forth, or since did from their ashes come.
Triumph, my Britain, thou hast one to show
To whom all scenes of Europe homage owe.
He was not of an age, but for all time!"

And here I abandon all my vanity to proclaim,

" a good poet's made as well as born.
And such wert thou. Look how the father's face
Lives in his issue, even so the race
Of Shakespeare's mind and manners brightly shines
In his well turned and true-filed lines:
In each of which he seems to shake a lance,
As brandished at the eyes of ignorance.
Sweet swan of Avon! what a sight it were
To see thee in our waters yet appear,
And make those flights upon the banks of Thames,
That did so take Eliza and our James!
But stay, I see thee in the hemisphere
Advanced, and made a constellation there:
Shine forth, thou Star of Poets, and with rage,
Or influence, chide or cheer the drooping stage,
Which, since thy flight from hence, hath mourned like
night,
And despairs day, but for thy volume's light."
(Jonson falls weeping disconsolately ….and then recovers
himself, to speak again.)

I know not whether I weep for a lost friend or that his
talent was not mine, even so the grief is real.
(pause)

And so we have this little play, a tribute in another way,
not of the standard I would ordain, but then again 'twas
hard enough for me to return, to say my piece that you
might learn, let alone to write another play, but there's a
little more I have to say. The author asks that I recite the
speech of Jacques which Will did write in his wondrous
play, which in its time was quite a hit, the play called As
You Like It. The play you are about to hear has seven
acts, not his idea but taken from the Bard himself, so
listen now and to all good health.

(in trenchant tones he recites)

All the world's a stage,
    And all the men and women merely players;
    They have their exits and their entrances;
    And one man in his time plays many parts,
    His acts being seven ages. At first the infant,
    Mewling and puking in the nurse's arms;
    Then the whining school-boy, with his satchel

And shining morning face, creeping like snail
Unwillingly to school. And then the lover,
Sighing like furnace, with a woeful ballad
Made to his mistress' eyebrow. Then a soldier,
Full of strange oaths, and bearded like the pard,
Jealous in honour, sudden and quick in quarrel,
Seeking the bubble reputation
Even in the cannon's mouth. And then the justice,
In fair round belly with good capon lin'd,
With eyes severe and beard of formal cut,
Full of wise saws and modern instances;
And so he plays his part. The sixth age shifts
Into the lean and slipper'd pantaloon,
 With spectacles on nose and pouch on side,
His youthful hose, well saved, a world too wide
 For his shrunk shank;
His big manly voice turning towards childish treble
pipes
 And whistles in his sound.
 Last scene of all,
  That ends this strange eventful history,
 Is second childishness and mere oblivion,
  Sans teeth, sans eyes, sans taste, sans everything.

(Jonson moves to the side of the stage under a softer light.

ACT 1.

Jonson (recites from the side of the stage, then retires)

The first Act….. "At first the infant,
Mewling and puking in the nurse's arms;"
We are at the Manor House, Wilmcote, on the
Estate of Robert Ardern, where Richard Shakespeare was
a tenant; it is early in the year of 1557.

(exit Jonson)

Scene 1.

Persons
Robert Arden
Richard Shakespeare
John Shakespeare
Mary Arden

Knocking upon the door, enter Richard and John; within
Robert and Mary.

Robert:	Welcome in Richard and John.
Richard:	Good day to you Robert and my dear Mary.
John:	Good day m'lord Arden, good day dear Mary.
Robert:	Gentlemen, over these many years you, Richard have been a loyal tenant. You know you have my friendship and respect.
Richard:	It is a lot that you have given and I fear it imposes deeply that through my son we ask for more from the Ardens.
Robert:	So good a friend need not think he does impose on this friendship.
John:	If I may m'lord be permitted, as you know and no doubt have noticed over these last few months, I have often sought the company of Mary.
Robert:	No man could be trusted more with my youngest daughter and she now of marriageable age. Albeit Alicia, a year above, remains a maiden also.
John:	Sir, it is my great desire to marry Mary and I humbly ask your permission for this contraction.

Robert:	Are you able to care for a wife John?
John:	Sir, I have left tending the land with my father here at Wilmcote these last few years to complete my trade as a whittawer and glover at Stratford and I believe that this will give ample means. What is more, I have leased two copy-hold houses in Stratford, one in Greenhill Street and a house in Henley Street.
Robert:	Mary, what do you say, do you love this man?
Mary:	Father, although ten years separate us, these last ten years I have changed from a girl to a woman and always has John been my fascination and gently has he treated my attention. You ask if I love him and I tell you all most sincerely that I have always loved him.
Robert:	None of this gives me surprise but these words confirm my own understanding; and what of you John, do you love my daughter.
John:	Sire, I think of nothing but my love for Mary and I do promise to always honour and cherish her if you will permit me to take her hand.
Robert:	You both have my blessing. So it shall be that the union of Arden and Shakespeare by land these past years shall be crowned with a union of flesh and blood and let the banns be proclaimed by our beloved vicar of Temple Grafton, the good Father John Frith. Upon you my dear Mary I will settle a small plot at Snitterton to enrich your dowry.
Mary:	My grateful thanks to you dear Father.
John:	I vouch my most sacred promise to you sire to love and cherish your daughter always and I thank you deeply for your kind blessing.
Robert:	Let us share a toast to these affied that their bent for each other may endure to the end of their days and let you two be wed before the year is done.

Takes a decanter and pours a goblet for each which they raise in toast each declaiming "Slainte".

Scene 2.

Jonson (recites from the side of the stage, then retires)

At the home of John and Mary Shakespeare at Henley Street, Stratford. It is mid-year 1563.

Exit Jonson

Persons.
Mary.
John.

John enters, Mary is sitting doing cross-stitch.

John	How is it with my darling wife.
Mary	I have some news.
John.	Pray let it be glad tidings.
Mary	I have been to Wilmcote to see the midwife and she tells me I am with another child.
John	Oh Mary, I am happy and pray to St. Winifred that it shall go well. Surely God must now smile on us having seen fit to take from us two children already when they were but babes.
Mary	I have wept many tears since the death of our two beautiful daughters and I have prayed to Mother Mary to send me a child with the vigour to live a long and happy life.
John	Aye, any child will need the strength of an Arden and the faith as well to withstand the testing of these times. The Holy Roman Church is condemned by the Tudors. Our Catholic faith has been criticized and we are told to worship as Protestants but then our faith as Catholics is revived only to have the Protestant reforms come back again.
Mary	The Tudors fight among themselves, so what are country folk like us to do? First a revolution started by Henry 8 and then his son Edward, in suit to his father's memory proclaims himself an ardent Protestant, and then his sister Mary restores our Catholic

faith, but we are shamed by her in burning Protestant martyrs .

John   There is blood everywhere. Mary our Catholic redeemer, shames us with killing 300 martyrs for their Protestant faith. I can have no more comfort from her life, than from her death.

Mary   And all done in the name of God!

John   What will our child encounter, the known ways are in such turmoil? Our new Queen has been through the fires of torture to take her crown and I know not what to think of her, nor what life will be like for us and our child.

Mary.   By my faith her Father cursed not only his own family but his people and their faith.

John.   Twenty four years of marriage to Catherine of Aragon and he demands the Holy Father annul it for lack of a male heir-apparent leaving her only surviving child our good Queen Mary. God forgive her.

Mary.   And now this new Queen, Elizabeth. What must she think? What of her faith when her father, the mad Henry 8 defies the Church to leave Catherine to marry Anne Boleyn? Does his sickening violence infect our new Queen? Elizabeth is but a young girl to have her mother beheaded by her father, for failing to bring the lunatic Henry a male heir!

John.   Aye marry! And then old Henry declares Elizabeth illegitimate and locks her in prison so ensuring his madness will dwell within her.

Mary.   Oh and her half sister, Mary Tudor for five years brought us back to the faith until the release of Henry's mad imprisoned spawn,her own sister. So fully formed to her father's madness, our new Queen Liz killed her own sister, the good Mary,in '58.

Mary   So from blood to blood we bring our child to a time of blood when the new Queen rules by killing her own sister.

John   We need not fear what is to come when we have our faith and the security of our hearth

	dear wife, Mary, we will prevail and bring some good to this evil world.
Mary.	I have prayed it will be so.

Scene 3.

Jonson (recites from the side of the stage, then retires)

The next scene finds itself at Holy Trinity Church , Stratford upon Avon, April 26, 1564

Exit Jonson

Persons.
Mary
John
Father John Frith.
Family and Friends present.

The Priest cradles the baby over the font.

Frith	Bring to me Guliermus filius Johannes Shakespeare.
Mary	(Handing the child to the priest) Father, my son, but two days old.
Frith	(The priest taking the child) William son of John and Mary Shakespeare. I baptise you in the name of the father, the son and the holy spirit. We thank you father for the water of baptism. May god who has received you by baptism into his flock pour upon you the riches of his grace. Amen.
All	Amen.

The child William is passed by the priest to Mary.

Frith	John, my hearty congratulations to you on the birth of your son, he is a spritely young boy with his grandfather Robert's eyes, how sad Robert has passed on and yet I feel in this young man there is the living spirit of the Ardens and the Shakespeares.
John	Thank you Father.
Frith	How goes your business in Stratford?

John	I have just bought a new house in Henley Street for Mary and our new son. I have had good fortune as a Master Glover and lately have been traveling with a new endeavour.
Frith	I have heard John that you have some dealings with wool yet I would not whisper a word lest you be called a brogger.
John	Well Father let us keep this to ourselves, let it be my informal confession to you that I have bought and sold some fleece outside the Queens' monopoly but the Lords themselves carry my wool in the weave of their cloaks and if the payment be right it seems the garment is often full enough to blind their eyes.
Frith	Well you take care in pulling the wool over their eyes for those that pardon you now would sell you out to a higher bidder before a pang of conscience or loyalty could protect you.
John.	Thank you good father and may God protect you too in these uncertain times.
Frith	True it is John, I never know from one day till the sun rises whether my next service will be at Holy Trinity or the Tower of London.
John	What make you of our new good Queen?
Frith	If not proclaiming our love for her highness. in good voice, it is better to speak in whispers, so wide do her army of spies spread around us. I fear she will be worse than her half-sister bloody Mary whom she dispatched in the name of her new Protestant God, but who through her truer faith will find a more certain home with our Lord.

Scene 4.

Jonson (recites from the side of the stage, then retires)

We are now at the home of John and Mary
Shakespeare at Henley Street. (late June
1564, William but two months old)

Exit Jonson

Persons.
Mary
John

Mary upon the bed with the child William asleep in the cradle.

Mary	Hush John running in here all agog and with so much puffing.
John	(whispers) Forgive me my dear I have come from the Guild Hall where the council are all in uproar over the plague.
Mary	Let little William sleep without o'hearing this talk, come to the corner so we can speak away from his hearing.
John	My love forgive me if my memories taunt you but when I heard this talk, tears flooded into my eyes remembering our first child dear Joan dying as a babe in your arms and then our beautiful Margareta just half a year with us and taken; and now a malignant fever is reported in the town, that same plague which ravaged London last year.
Mary	How does it show John?
John	It came from London with a traveler and has already felled two in Stratford and I fear its violence which has done great harm in London.
Mary	What are we to do?
John	You and William must haste back to Snitterfield until it is safe and I will do what I can with the businesses in between.
Mary	I don't want to be without you, my beloved husband.
John	Mary we could not bear the loss of another child and I will not be far away and will come to Snitterfield whenever I can but with care lest I should bring the pestilence with me.
Mary	You are right (looking into the cradle) I thank God for this our living child, for you and for the privilege of refuge from our

	house in town, please don't think me ungrateful. God bless my late father who left me the house in Snitterfield.
John	Mary, whilst the child sleeps, pack at once and then I will hie thee to our country home and in penance for our good fortune in having refuge, I will pledge one shilling and six pence to the relief of the poor.

ACT 2.

Jonson (recites from the side of the stage, then retires)

The Second Act…..."Then the whining school-boy, with his satchel
   And shining morning face, creeping like snail
   Unwillingly to school"
This scene finds us At the Guild Hall in Stratford (4th July 1565)

Exit Jonson.

Scene 1.

Persons.
Mary Shakespeare
Young William
John Shakespeare
The Town Clerk of Stratford
The Aldermen Assembled

The Clerk:	I call upon John Shakespeare of Stratford upon Avon in respect of whom in recognition of his service in the past as town constable, juryman leet and affeeror, is to take oath as Alderman of the Queens' Borough of Stratford.
John.	In answer to the call, I John Shakespeare present myself to be so bound. (Takes the Bible)

The Clerk	Do you, John Shakespeare, swear and utterly testify and declare in your conscience that the queen's highness is the only supreme governor of this realm and of all other her highness's dominions and countries, as well in all spiritual or ecclesiastical things or causes as temporal?
John	So help me God and by the contents of this Book
Clerk	In accordance with the provisions of the Act of Uniformity of 1559 I can pronounce you, John Shakespeare, Alderman of the Borough of Stratford and servant to her Majesty Queen Elizabeth.
John	Fellow Council members and my Lord Mayor, I call upon you as my guests to come to our home in Henley Street to celebrate with me, my wife Mary,and young William, this great honour which has been conferred upon me.

Guests shuffle away:

Mary	(aside to John nursing young William) You know I love you my husband but in taking that oath you have forsaken our faith in the Holy Catholic Church.
John	Mary, I am not running for Sainthood, and I think it better that those of the faith take office to maintain protection of their own; don't you agree? I do not like these times, it is as though we are on a wagon tearing down a road leading we know not where with the horses loose of their reins. We are led to believe that her highness will practise clemency and reconciliation with the old faith; and while that is so, I remain master of this situation though it would be arrogant to say I am comfortable with it, or that we can count on it.
Mary	I am not separate from you on this, but I am fearful and I feel a great allegiance to our own people who are now on the descent.
John	I understand Mary but let us push on as best we can and do whatever we can for our own, a false oath to this mad woman brings no judgment upon us.

Scene 2.

Jonson (recites from the side of the stage, then retires)

It is the First Thursday before Easter, 1568. This scene finds itself at Coventry on The Feast Day of Corpus Christi when the local guildmen perform the Mystery Plays presented every year for three days around the festival. The Shakespeare's, with Mary pregnant, have come with young William almost four years old.

Jonson retires

Persons.
John
Mary (is pregnant in the second trimester)
William

Mary	You take young William to the town square for the plays and I will join you when I am able, I feel so ill with this pregnancy.
William	Mother, father and I will carry you, you can't miss the story of the Flood.
Mary	And tell me William what would you know
of the Flood.	
John	Aye Mary, you know I have little reading and as for writing I rely on the shire scribe to record my dealings in council and the tote men for my wool, but here in our young William we have a veritable scholar, for I saw him reading aloud from the Bible given us by Father Frith.
Mary	Is it true William are you reading about Noah.
William	Oh yes mother and more besides.
John	It confounds me how this boy proceeds, he'll be writing next.

Mary	I am at a loss for I have been reading to him the Aesops Fables and he asks me of words and seems to have taught himself.
William	Mother, I love reading and Noah was a good man.
Mary	Indeed William, Noah was good and where did you learn about Noah?
William	I am reading Genesis and I know what the Lord said, he said "I will destroy man whom I have created from the face of the Earth, " but he liked Noah, and in the Bible its says that Noah "found grace in the eyes of the Lord."
John	Oh William (laughing) what is grace?
William	It means Father that he had the blessing of the Lord.
John	(to Mary) The boy runs ahead of us all, I'll be blessed.
William	And then "the Lord said, unto Noah come thou and all thy house into the Ark ; for thee have I seen righteous before me in this generation."
Mary	(To John) I believe our son has said that verbatim from the Holy Scripture of Genesis.
William	"And it rained for forty days and nights and only Noah and his wife and family and two of every creature were alive."
John	Harken, young William move over here to the window and let us stay with Mother and watch, for the cart is coming and it is as high as our roof, look there.
William	(to the window) Oh mother can you hear it, I can see the pageant cart, and it is like a small hill covered in pretty ribbons and there is Noah and he is standing in the ark, and there are the animals! Oh and Noah has a big beard and he is shaking his staff and about to speak!
The Players	(sound through the window)

Noah: Forty days and nights of pouring rain,

Till no living thing on sodden land
remains.I'll send this crow a-flying to
seek out land.
A place where all aboard might stand.

William   Mother do you hear Noah and he has loosed
a crow and it has flown to the roof across the
square.

John   It is make-believe William, the crow will be
home by and by.
Mary   Do not query the boy's imagination so John!
John   Wait, Noah speaks again!

Noah: This crow has flown to eat dead meat,
A more faithful messenger will I send.
Fly out fair dove across the sea,
Bring us some token of the flooding's end.

William   Mother, Father, he has a dove in his hand and
off it flies. It is circling us now, oh, and now it
has gone.
John   Yes Mary the dove has hied himself yonder
(winking to Mary) but he'll be back young Will,
keep your eye towards Noah. (aside to Mary) I
think Noah has a pretty young lass at the back of
the cart to see to that .
Willam   Mother, mother, can you come to see this, quick
mother, a young girl brings back the dove and
carries withal a branch .

Noah: Oh joyous day the dove dost bring,
A sprig of olive bush on the wing.
We give our praise to our Lord God above
And kneel in thanks for his faithful love.

William   Mother mother I love these plays, it is just
as I imagined Noah and the ark to be; did
you know how old Noah was when he had
to build the ark?
Mary   Well I suppose he must have been an older
man because he had three sons and they
were married.
William.   Three sons and they had three wives.
Mary   Well then he was an oldish man but did he
have grandchildren?

William	He must have had many mother, for in the bible I read that he was six hundred years old and after the flood he got drunk on his wine and grew angry with Canaan, the son of his son Ham and he lived for another 350 years.
Mary	William you have been learning a lot from Father Frith's Bible and that will profit you much .
William	I love those stories almost as much as Aesop's.
John	Well there is a time for reading and there is a time for feasting and reveling, how goes it Mary, are you well enough to come to the revels.
Mary	(Rising) I feel a little better, I was weary with the travel but the music and the playing has lifted me so let us go together.
John.	Put on your cloak young William for the autumn wind still chills.(he puts the cloak around William and assists Mary to her feet)
Mary	Tarry a moment while I brush my hair and you two tidy yourselves a little, and you John, you are not a country boy nor just an Alderman, but Bailiff of Stratford, so straighten your suit and smooth your hose and look the part.
John	Come on Bill, let us shake ourselves down as gentlemen must, but first it is the son of the Bailiff who mussed, so mussed you will be! Tidy your hair young fellow (he musses young William's hair in play)
William	(Takes up his mother's hair brush and parries towards his father as with a sword) Do not trifle with a Knight's hair thou varlet!
John	(Feigning horror) What cruel words from this baby Knight to his old father, I'll teach him how to use a sword. (He takes William up in play, puts him across his knee and paddy wacks him with the brush).
Mary	Alright, come on you two jousting Knights, the pageant is moving on so let's hie to the street to join the revels.

(John puts William down again, but musses his hair yet again and the boy punches playfully at his father's leg, then clutches to it.

Mary leads out of the room and John attempts to leave but has young William with his arm wrapped around is leg slowing his departure; they all leave in this fashion)

They leave the Inn room for the revels.

Scene 3.

Jonson (recites from the side of the stage, then retires)

This scene finds itself at the Grammar School, Stratford.1573. William started school when he was 7 as was the custom, and during the hours from 6.30 in the morning until 7 at night was drilled in grammar, and the new godliness of Protestantism, Latin, Greek and drama. By all accounts he loved being a scholar. He is now 9 years old.

Jonson retires.

Persons.
William (now aged 9)
Mr. Hunt (teacher)
(other pupils)

Hunt:	Shortly boys we will break for lunch but before we take our repast I wish to remind you of the way we deal with the agent after a passive verb; Shakespeare, turn the active sentence Antony blames Brutus into Latin.
William	Antonius Brutum culpat, sir?
Hunt	Well done William. Now suppose we make the same statement in the passive, William are you able to assist the class?
William	Brutus culpatur sir?
Hunt	Yes, but boys how are we to deal with the agent? Not simply by putting him into the ablative because as we have learned

whether the verb is active or passive, the ablative is used to denote the instrument with which, not the person by whom, a thing is done, so Brutus is blamed by Antony turns into Brutus ab Antonio culpatur. So let us go back to William, Caesar is praised by Antony, blamed by Brutus, is?

William   Is it Caesar ab Antonio laudatur, a Bruto culpatur?

Hunt   Well done William. Now boys you can go for lunch and when we return this afternoon you will be performing for your parents so review your parts and enjoy the revels for the rest of today. William will you wait a moment so that I might speak with you.

Other boys file out quietly, one pushing between William and Mr. Hunt who chides him.

Hunt   Loomes, a beg pardon young man.

Loomes   Beg pardon sir.

Hunt   William, I have not kept you back to punish you so set your mind at rest; on the contrary I am delighted with your progress. You appear to be enjoying your classes and studying hard at your Latin.

William   Sir, I fear I have small Latin and less Greek and yet I love learning Latin, because through it I can learn more about the writers.

Hunt   Which writers have your interest William?

William   I like reading Plautus' plays because they are amusing and tell good stories about people. I want to write plays like Plautus.

Hunt   Well this afternoon you are in a play about Ralph Royster Doyster, do you like that play?

William   Indeed I do sir, very much and it reminds me of Miles Gloriousus by Plautus.

Hunt   Is that so, well that is not a coincidence. Do you know who wrote Royster Doyster?

William   Yes sir, Master Nicholas Udall.

Hunt   That is right William, Nicholas Udall, he was a Master at Eton and before his sad

	demise he was a Court poet for Good Queen Mary. He loved Plautus and I agree with you, that his comedy Royster Doyster is founded on Plautus play Miles Gloriousus.
William	I thought so sir, when I was learning my part in the play I was reminded continually of Miles Gloriousus.
Hunt	What other writers in Latin do you fancy William?
William	Sir, I love Publius Ovidius Naso.
Hunt	Are you reading him in Latin?
William	Mainly sir, however I must confess to reading the english translation by Arthur Golding.
Hunt	And is there anything in particular of Ovid's that you love?
William	I often read his poems of exile sir, and they make me feel so sad.
Hunt	Why so sad?
William	Well sir, to think of the greatest poet of Rome relegated in exile to Tomis with no-one to understand or listen to him.
Hunt	Yes, that was very sad, and perhaps a lesson to be learned in that.
William	He offended the Emperor and his talents were sent where they would not likely be heard.
Hunt	Fortunately Will, he has been heard and continues to be and they weren't just poems of Exile.
William	Oh you mean the love poems.
Hunt	Well yes, but they aren't on the curriculum yet.
William	Oh well, ahem, yes sir.
Hunt	Well you run on to lunch now William and I will see you in the afternoon at your play.
William	The Lord's Prayer Story.
Hunt	What on earth do you mean?
William	Oh sorry sir, I like playing with words and I made that out of the letters to Ralph Royster Doyster.
Hunt	Is that so, well you had better go and rest your brain now and have some lunch and I will see you anon.
William	Thank you sir.

William leaves the classroom.
Enter another teacher Aspinall.

Hunt.	Aspinall, you've come to fetch me for lunch.
Aspinall	It is an uncommonly fine day and I thought we could go to the inn for some pie and ale.
Hunt	What a fine suggestion.
Aspinall	I see you were in conversation with young Master Shakespeare, he is an extraordinary student in my Greek classes.
Hunt	I am astounded at the prodigious talent of that young fellow. Do you know he already has enough Latin to be reading Plautus' plays in the original text, well enough to eke out comparisons with Udall's Royster Doyster and the little fellow has extended his education with the erotic works of Ovid.
Aspinall	I am not surprised, I have never encountered a student with such a thirst for learning and it is a good sign that he is developing an interest through our beloved Ovid in other matters than books.
Hunt	Well speaking of thirst, let us go and slake ours before the sun descends.
	They leave.

ACT 3

Jonson (recites from the side of the stage, then retires)

The third act …..
"And then the lover,
Sighing like furnace, with a woeful ballad
Made to his mistress' eyebrow."

It is 1578, and young William is now 14 years old and this scene finds itself at the Shakespeare's house at Henley Street in Stratford. William now has a brother and two sisters. They are Gilbert (William's brother now aged 11) Joan (William's sister, now aged 9) and Anne (William's sister, now aged 7). His parents have already lost two other children in infancy, and Anne has only a year to live.

Exit Jonson

Scene 1.

Persons.

John
Mary
William
Gilbert
Joan
Anne

Mary   (busy about the table holding papers)
Enter John

John   What have you there Mary, it can't be good news
              but fortunately unlike me, you can read.
Mary   It is some form of legal document for you from the
              Queens Men, but I cannot understand the Latin.
John   I've just come from the borough hall when we had
              to answer an order of the council to pay six
              shillings and eight pence for the furniture of three
              pikemen, two billmen and one archer.
Mary   My Lord, we cannot afford it John.
John   I know Mary, and there is a contribution to be
              made weekly for the relief of the poor, and
              although I am not just an alderman but head
              alderman I had to ask to be excepted because of
              our circumstances, and the humiliation is still
              hurting me.
Mary   You cannot pay what you don't have nor can you
              deprive the children. It is with William, Gilbert
              ,Joan and Anne where your charity must begin.
John   I know Mary, I am crestfallen that just four years
              ago, I could pay forty pounds to the Hall's to buy
              us more property in Henley Street, but now my
              fortune has turned.
Mary   It is not the fates that daunt us John but the
              Queen's audit.
John   Aye, the wool market has fallen to pieces and
              although I had my secret supplies and kept
              brogging outside the Queens' monopoly, her spies
              are everywhere and there is no trading to be done
              now for fear of ruin.

Mary	There is the Glovers Shop, we still have that.
John	Aye we do my dear lass, but there is little money in gloving in good times and now money is so strict there won't be enough to feed ourselves and the children.
Mary	What about the school fees and little Anne to start next year?
John	I have decided Gilbert and Joan can continue, and we will find money for Anne; but William will have to leave and take to the trade with me.
Mary	What if we sell some land, I have the parcel in Snitterfield that my father gave me, we must do something; his Masters tell me Will is uncommon clever and could study at University.
John	I am sorry Mary even if we sell all but our home we can still barely pay the debts that I have; lest I be sent to prison, it is a matter of no choice but I do not relish telling him.
Mary	I will pray to God and seek blessing at Mass for our family.
John	Even in that silent resort we must be careful, the talk around the alderman is that the Queen is planning to banish the Latin Mass and allow only the reformed church to preach.
Mary	It cannot be so, the Holy Father would never permit it.
John	You forget what Elizabeth's father had to say to the Holy Father and what she herself has done to her own sister.

Enter William, Gilbert and Joan

Mary	Children are you weary from your long day at school?
William	It is not too hard in these summer days mother; we leave in the light and return in the light but in winter it is dark to dark.
Mary	And what did you learn today children?
Joan	Well mother, we learned about Jesus and the Sermon on the Mount and then we had our Latin lesson, and later we did some drawing and then we did some play acting.
Mary	Well you go and wash up now and we will have some supper, give me a cuddle for your trouble; and you Gilbert, what filled your day?

Gilbert	After breakfast Mr. Aspinall took us to the Avon river and we met some sailors from Her Majesty's Navy as part of our history lessons about the French and the Spanish fleets.
Mary	What an interesting day!
Gilbert	And then at lunch I won a handful of marbles which I can trade, here look at these (produces a cloth bag).
Mary	Gilbert you follow Joan and wash before supper; William, have you been enjoying yourself as much as the others?
William	Not quite as much excitement mother because I am studying for my examinations. Master Hunt says that should my results warrant he will submit my name for entrance to study letters at Cambridge.
John	Well, Will you know we are so proud of you especially in that your mother and I are country folk and I am unlettered and your mother can read only little.
William	I never think of you my dear parents as unlettered, all my wit and all I am, I owe to you both.
John	That is truly kind of you my fine son, but I have bad news.
William	What is it father?
John	Could you help us first Will by reading these papers to your mother and I but do it quietly so the others don't hear?
William	(Taking the papers handed to him by his mother) "By the Queens' order, John Shakespeare of Stratford is commanded to appear before Her Majesty's Justice to answer for the debt of five pounds due and owing to one Roger Sadler, Esquire, baker, in default of which levy will be made upon his sureties, Edmund Lambert and Cornishe." It is a summons for moneys due and owing Father.
John	I feared as much and what is worse Will, your mother and I cannot pay it and from what you read it must mean that the law will chase my good friends and backers Lambert and Cornishe.

William	I believe that is what it proposes Father.
Mary	Well that is it, I have decided we must sell the two tenements which Father willed to me at Snitterfield.
John	Mary, I confess that they have been promised already but the best price I can gather is four pounds!
Mary	Then we must sell more.
William	What can I do Father, to help?
John	Will, I hope you will forgive me son, because there is nothing more that your mother and I wanted than to fulfill your promise by getting you the best schooling ; I am ashamed to tell you that I cannot afford to keep you in the Grammar School and all I can offer is an apprenticeship at our Glovers.
William	Father you must not be ashamed, that is a very kind offer to take me as your apprentice, and then when I have my own trade and income, perhaps then, I will go back to finish my education.
Mary	Oh William, I know what this means to you and I am so sorry dear son (begins to cry).
William	Forbear to weep dearest mother, I know you and Father have given your best for all your children and look what I have learned, a little Greek, a little Latin and I can read whilever I have eyes and books to enjoy.
John	Well son, you go and ready for supper and God bless you.
William	Thank you father and dearest mother and for my sake do not think of these things as forever, there is much time before forever.

The light fades on Mary and John and William walks to the edge of the stage and falls to his knees and weeps.

Scene 2.
Jonson (recites from the side of the stage, then retires)

It is Mid year, 1580. William is 16 years old and this scene takes us to the Shakespeare's Glover's Shop in Stratford.

Exit Jonson

Persons.
John
William
Asaheurus Fromanteel (tradesman)
Two Soldiers

Asaheurus	What are you doing with that leather around your shoulders Will, are you day-dreaming again?
Will	"This mantle I just now stole from my wife inside there, and aha, it's going to a wench. This is the way to do it; to cheat a cunning jailer in such clever style! I have taken booty from the enemy without loss to my allies!"
Asaheurus	What on earth?
William	Well my dear , Urea Has Us, that is from Plautus' play the Menaechmi, and you must know that whatever the play if it be writ by Plautus or Seneca there can be no better.
Asaheurus	I'll not argue the point will, but why do you call me Urea Has Us?
William	You must forgive my word play Asaheurus, I can't help playing with the letters, you know I Am Will?
Asaheurus	Yes, of course I know you are Will?
William	No, you see if you play the letters of William is becomes I Am Will.
Asaheurus	I see what you mean, I sometimes do that; what do you make of Shakespeare?
William	Keeps a share, he's a speaker, he see a spark.
Asaheurus	You are running ahead of me young Will, just rest that brain a while and cut me out a chevron of kid hide.

Enter John

John	How is the trade today my boys?
Asaheurus	No-one has been in buying but we have been cutting the order for Coventry.
John	(moves to close the door, and speaks in a hushed tone) Gather around boys; It needs that I whisper to you both. You know our sacred mass is

26

	being challenged by Queen Bess and the faith which we all share is a slave to the reforms, well the Holy Father has sent messengers to us and even now they are hiding on our shores.
Asaheurus	You know I am staunch to our Church John, what is to be done?
John	Remember no-one outside our number is to be trusted and here there are lives at stake.
William	Has it come to this?
John	Aye Will, I have had to resign from the Council lest I would utterly forsake my faith; already I have had to compromise to keep my office. I have been the Queens' representative these last years in Stratford and have at times felt like a Judas, painting over our religious history in the borough chambers with whitewash to comply with her edicts; that matters little, the pictures remain but she would have had them destroyed.
William	Who comes as the Pope's emissary?
John	Edmund Campion has come bringing with him a contract, the Testament of the Soul for all the faithful. He comes with the Jesuits to travel in secret to speak with the faithful and by my patron Saint Winifred I will assist them even if it cost my life; I do not ask that of either of you, but I do ask your strict silence on these matters, and where there is little risk, to assist me?
Asaheurus	As my friend and Master Glover you have my word and my silence.
William	And I Father would die before betraying you.
John	Both of you have to understand that the loyalty extends beyond fathers, brothers, sisters, children and the like, for the very faith is under siege, and now the Holy Father has declared the taking of communion in the reformed church to be a mortal sin. He has excommunicated Queen Bess and she in turn has declared war on the Holy See.
Asaheurus	Are you at risk?

John	I have taken some Jesuits in secret to our friends the Grants and others have gone to the Catesby's in Lancashire; the Royal spies are everywhere and their hounds are baying for Catholic blood.

Knocking on the Door.

John	Beware, hide anything which betrays your faith and even on pain of death speak none of this.

Opens Door

Two Soldiers Enter.

Soldier 1	Which of you is John Shakespeare?
John	I am John Shakespeare, you need not bother my apprentices.
Soldier 1	You are under arrest.

Second Soldier steps forward and takes John by the arm.

John	By whose command do you detain me?
Soldier	By the Queens own command you are to be taken to London to answer the charge that you did attend a forbidden pilgrimage to the shrine of St. Winifred of Holy Well.
William	What madness?
Soldier 1	Watch your tongue son or you will join your Master for sedition.
John	Hold fast Will, I shall return by and by; let your mother know I am gone briefly.

The Soldiers lead John Shakespeare away.

William	This Queen was once a bastard called, and it did seem a cruel description for one so young but she does earn it now.
Asaheurus	Careful Will, you are rightly angry but in these times it won't profit your family for you to be locked away. Your Father knows the ways of the world and will survive his inquisition, you look to your tongue and, find another way about that won't attract the spying worms.

William	Methinks it is in the poets' field that all I feel can be revealed.
Asaheurus	That is right Will, there's nothing you can do now, just go to your mother and let the word out that they have John.
William	(Aside) "For she hath no exchequer now but his, And proud of many, lives upon his gains? O him she stores, to show what wealth she had, In days long since, before these last so bad."
Asaheurus	What was that Will?
William	Oh, it is part of a sonnet I have written, alas it tells too much. I will be off Asaheurus to take the news to my family.
Asaheurus	God speed and may he care for you and your family Will.

Scene 3.

Jonson (recites from the side of the stage, then retires)

This scene finds itself at Shottery, a village not far from Stratford, where William had become acquainted with the daughter of one of his Father's business partners. It is midyear 1582 .William's father had escaped the predations of Elizabeth's inquisitors and William was courting. Anne waits by the village Well and William strides up, he is now 18.

Exit Ben Jonson

Persons.
William
Anne Hathaway

Anne	Will, you have come as you promised.

William	I could not wait until father closed up for the day to see you, I have run the mile here and am so happy to be with you I scarce am tired.
Anne	It is a mild evening do you want to walk with me to the Shottery brook.
William	I have just passed through there and it is quiet and peaceful and the perfect place to walk.

They wander along hand in hand along the stage and
back again and so forth.

William   (recites to Anne)
    The day was sultry, and past its middle hour,
    The sun came warm and yellow through the
    shutter,
    The other lay closed against the heat,
    It was a twilight that lights the sides of trees,
    And then Corinna comes, old she's not, young
    Her tunic unbelted, her soft dark hair,
    Into the warmth of the room she'd barely stepp'd
    When I tore the tunic from her
    As she struggled to keep it about her
    But she was conquered without difficulty
    Coyly and willingly in that half light.
    I let her stand before me and
    Upon her body there was not a blemish
     How fit for caresses her beautiful sides,
     And her arms, her neck, her breasts,
     And these I did touch gently,
     Tempering my fever to go about her,
     Knowing this moment was reverential,
     Her thighs were soft and white,
     And I did feel them with my cheeks,
     And it was like the beginning and
     The end of all days,
     I saw nothing that I could not praise
      And I clasped her, naked as she was
     Close to my body

Anne	Did you write that Will?
William	No it is from Ovid in his book Amores.
Anne	And why do you quote it to me?
William	Because you are so beautiful it captures my dreams of you that keep me awake at night.

Anne	I cannot be like Corinna, I am a country girl with country manners.
William	You know your country leaves, but seriously you are my Corinna, Anne.
Anne	William you are cheeky with your words, but I love you for it. Be serious for a moment; you are but eighteen years old, you are just a man and I am twenty seven and love has passed me by, and, well, fate has deemed to take my early love away.
William	And you will love again, do you not love me?
Anne	When you were just apprenticed in your Father's shop I was already in my twenties and the family despaired then that I should ever be a wife and mother.
William	Well, now is your chance again Anne for I want you more than any other.
Anne	Has there been any other?
William	I have not had time for any other and even when I was a lad I lusted for you but could not declare my love until you would accept me as a serious suitor.
Anne	Well is that true? I suppose you are now a serious suitor, certainly my friends tease me about your frequent visits to our home.
William	I am serious Anne, never more so. I am young but not foolish and I have dreams for what I will become.
Anne	What dreams do you have?
William	I dream of being a playwright, of penning works like Plautus and Seneca, of having the audiences roll about at my stories or weep like babies when I change the mood from glad to sadness.
Anne	Is that what you are doing with me, sweeping me up like an audience to leave me alone when your play is done?
William	My love for you is more intense and needful than my lust, which I do confess.
Anne	I know your lust and would say I have yielded to it, were it not that my own desire exceeds yours; but we need proceed no further than the affairs of our present arrangement.

William	Do not send me away when my love needs your constant company.
Anne	Let us speak plainly Will, I am your elder by some years and though you are my fancy and you are mad for me now, you know little of the world beyond Stratford.
William	I have come to learn more than I should know. You and your family know what we of the faith endure under Elizabeth. My father arrested and just spared. I am, I know, a young clown at times, but my heart is a deep well with many sad memories saturating me, the loss of my dear sister Anne, the proscription of our faith, all of these things set my mind to thought. In the midst of this Anne I often think too deeply and feel alone, except when I am with you, do not send me away.
Anne	I know Will, I do not mean to mock your feelings but have you considered mine. I do love you, I marvel at your learning and my heart beats every time I see you, I cannot understand my own feelings. There are farmers more my age who seek my hand but I hate them all.
William	Do you hate me?
Anne	No not you. I only think of you. I ask you to tell me where would it lead us?
William	We are all, whatever age, heading to the same place dear Anne, our faith tells us where, but in truth I know not for sure, all I can devote myself to are those who travel with me- and you are my closest and dearest. Will you give in to my will and travel with me?
Anne	I vouch in my head I am unsure but in my heart I have no doubt that there will never be another one like you, for me and so I will travel with you Will.

(They embrace)

Scene 4.

Jonson (recites from the side of the stage, then retires)

     Will was always full of enthusiasm, and no more so than in his courtship with Anne, for our next scene finds us on Tues Nov 27, 1582 at Worcester Cathedral , Anne was pregnant and they needed a marriage licence.

Exit Jonson

Persons.

William
Anne
Father Frith

Frith	Young people you cannot have the banns and marry during the six weeks of Christmas so it might be that you are a little late.
William	Father, we have more need than the law will allow and being of the old Faith I hoped to importune you to issue a marriage licence. I have with me a bond in forty pounds from my friends Fulk Sandells and John Richardson and a consent of Anne's brother bearing the father's seal.
Frith	Well young Will, you do ask a lot, which I must confess I admire in you, but when you make such a proposition be sure to do it with whispers; you of all people should know of our good Queen's inquisitors and the spies under every flagstone.
William	Oh yes, I do good Father, forgive me, I vouch my silence.
Frith	That is understood Will, I trust you completely and please give my warm regards to your Father, and to your brother. (turning to Anne). Anne, may your parents

	rest in peace. How say your brother about this arrangement?
Anne	Well Father, as you might see from my belly we announced our betrothal in a very certain manner and without apparent misgiving my brother has signed the consent which Will gave you under our late father's seal!
Frith	Indeed Anne, and I take it you were cajoled by young Will's endearing ways?
Anne	I match his wit every bit with experience good Father.
William	I'll admit Father that my fancies are more giddy and infirm but my purpose is sworn.
Frith	I believe Anne you are more than a match for young Will. Well let's about it. I will issue the licence and publish the banns instantly and you can marry in three days' time. I will do this without proclaiming or publishing the banns three times as her Majesty decrees, I have no time for her reformation anyway and in this we join the conspiracy together; but Will, I will make a mistake with Anne's surname, it would not be noble to implicate her beyond her present commitment.
Will	Thank you Father, call her Anna Whateley of Temple Grafton and should anyone scour the records they will spend their pointless time pursuing a wife who did never exist and I am upon my bond to complete this union.
Frith	Here Anne, sign Anne Whateley here next to Will's name and I will seal your licence and make the necessary certification of the publishing of the banns.
Anne	Thank you Father.
Frith	Bless you both and your child to be and see you in three days at St. Andrews, 30th November 1582.

(Three days later, at St. Andrews church 30th November 1582)

Present
William

Anne
Robert Hathaway (Anne's brother)
John Shakespeare
Mary Shakespeare
Father Frith
 Asaheurus Fromanteel (Will's best man)

(William stands by the altar with Father Frith)

Frith	I welcome our fair bride, Anne Hathaway. Enter Anne with her brother.
Frith	I read today from Ecclesiastes, Chapter 9 Verses 4, 9 and 10: For to him that is joined to all the living there is hope: for a living dog is better than a dead lion. Live joyfully with the wife whom thou lovest all the days of the life of thy vanity, which he hath given thee under the sun, all the days of thy vanity, for that is thy portion in this life, and in thy labour which thou takest under the sun. Whatsoever thy hand findeth to do, do it with thy might, for there is no work, nor device nor knowledge, nor wisdom in the grave wither thou goest. This is the word of the Lord.
All	Amen
Frith	Dearly beloved, we are gathered together here in the sight of God to join together this Man and this Woman in holy Matrimony; which is an honourable estate, instituted of God in Paradise, and into which holy estate these two persons present come now to be joined. Therefore if any man can shew any just cause, why they may not lawfully be joined together, by God's Law, or the Laws of the Realm; let him now speak, or else hereafter forever hold his peace. I require and charge you William and Anne , as ye will answer at the dreadful day of judgment when the secrets of all hearts shall be disclosed, that if either of you know any impediment, why ye may not be lawfully joined together in Matrimony, that

ye confess it. For ye be well assured, that so many as be coupled together otherwise than God's Word doth allow are not joined together by God; neither is their Matrimony lawful.

William, wilt thou have this Woman to be thy wedded wife, to live together after God's ordinance in the holy estate of Matrimony? Wilt thou love her, comfort her, honour, and keep her, in sickness and in health; and forsaking all others, keep thee only unto her, so long as ye both shall live?

William   I will.

Frith   Anne, wilt thou have this man to be thy wedded husband, to live together after God's ordinance in the holy estate of Matrimony? Wilt thou obey him, and serve him, love, honour, and keep him in sickness and in health; and, forsaking all others, keep thee only unto him, so long as ye both shall live?

Anne   I will.

Frith   Thus ends the formal betrothal.

(Father Frith then leads the couple to the Altar and takes the ring from Anne's brother and lays them on the bible)

Frith   Bless these Rings, O merciful Lord, that those who wear them, that give and receive them, may be ever faithful to one another, remain in your peace, and live and grow old together in your love, under their own vine and fig tree, and seeing their children's children. Amen.

(Father Frith takes the one ring and hands it to William)

William   (Places the ring on Anne's thumb (sic) and says) With this ring I thee wed, and with my body I thee honor, (then places it upon her index finger) and with all my worldly goods I thee endow; (then places it upon her ring finger) In the Name of the Father, and of the Son, and of the Holy Spirit. Amen.

(William and Anne then kneel before the Father)

Frith   Let us pray.. O Eternal God, Creator and Preserver of all mankind, Giver of all spiritual grace, the Author of everlasting life; Send thy blessing upon these thy servants, this man and this woman, whom we bless in thy Name; that, as Isaac and Rebecca lived faithfully together, so these persons may surely perform and keep the vow and covenant betwixt them made, whereof this Ring given and received is a token and pledge, and may ever hereafter remain in perfect love and peace together, and live according to thy laws; through Jesus Christ our Lord. Amen.

All   Amen

(Father Frith then joins Williams right hand to Anne's right hand

Frith   Those whom God hath joined together let no man put asunder. Forasmuch as William and Anne have consented together in holy wedlock, and have witnessed the same before God and this company, and thereto have given and pledged their troth each to the other, and have declared the same by giving and receiving of a Ring, and by joining of hands; I pronounce therefore that they be Man and Wife together, in the Name of the Father, and of the Son, and of the Holy Spirit. Amen

(Father Frith then turns from the altar)
Frith   You may kiss each the other.

(William and Anne embrace and then proceed from the Altar.)

(Anne then lays roses before a Statue of the Virgin Mary)

ACT 4.

Scene 1
Jonson (recites from the side of the stage, then retires)

The Fourth Act....Then a soldier,
   Full of strange oaths, and bearded like the pard,
   Jealous in honour, sudden and quick in quarrel,
   Seeking the bubble reputation
   Even in the cannon's mouth.

   It is 26 May 1583 only five or so months since the
wedding and we are at Henley Street in Stratford.

Exit Jonson.

Persons.

Midwife
William
Anne
John Shakespeare
Mary Shakespeare
Gilbert (William's younger brother)

(Sound of moaning from the adjoining room as Anne
gives birth)

Enter midwife speaks to William sitting with his parents
Mary and John.

Midwife	(Enters in haste) Would you come and assist Ma'am it's a difficult birth I fear.
Mary	I'll come at once.
John	You've found yourself in a family way young Will and 19 years of age, and you know that you cannot at law remain my apprentice, 'tis barred to married men, and that's a fact can no longer be concealed with this birth.
William	Master Cottam from the Grammar School has found me a position teaching in the Catholic way at Lancashire and if needs must I'll go there to support my wife and children.

John	You're a good lad Will, and proud of you I am. You know your family will always have a home under our roof and so shall remain until you need it no more, but if there's work in the offing you'll have to take it boy and see where it leads.
Midwife	(Returns) You may go to Mary now Will, a father to a bonnie daughter.
William	How is Anne?
Midwife	She's a healthy country girl Will, you go to her, she awaits.
	(Will and midwife leave and go to Anne)

Enter Mary

John	How is't , a healthy heifer?
Mary	Oh, John it is more than that, we are grandparents to a beautiful baby girl. Let's break out that special mead and celebrate.
John	(Goes to the cupboard to take out the mead and is commencing to pour a glass.)

Enter Gilbert

John	Hi Ho, it's uncle Gilbert.
Gilbert	Anne's been delivered of her child, is it a boy or a girl?
Mary	You have a niece Gilbert and a beautiful one at that.
Gilbert	That is good news mother and father but I fear I have come with a message that will balance our joy.
Mary	What news?
Gilbert	Your brother sent his valet to our shop and entreated me to tell no-one but you and father. Your brother's son in law, John Summerville has been arrested by the Queen's spies and taken to the tower.
Mary	Oh, Lord protect our family, how can this be?
Gilbert	He was overhead whilst drinking at an Inn in Buckinghamshire where he did declare Elizabeth an heretic whom he proposed to kill. No sooner had he slept the liquor off than he was taken by force to London and the valet says the inquisitors are seeking warrants for your brother's arrest as well.

Mary	Oh not Edward, John what can we do to stop this?
John	They've had me there Mary, and without proof he must be released as was I.
Mary	But John Summerville is a loud lad and what if it be proved that he did declare the Queen an heretic?
John	Then though it be the truth the ruthless witch will have him hanged drawn and quartered, she feasts on such shows.
Mary	But what of my brother Edward?
John	How can he be implicated Mary, unless he uttered the words as well, your Family has high standing and the Queen would be at risk to falsely charge him.
Mary	I pray to the Virgin for them all.

Enter William

William	Hi ho Gilbert, I am a father of a daughter, whom we call Susanna, and you my great brother in honour thereof, I dub thee Uncle Gilbert; but wait, where is the merriment and joy?
Gilbert	Forgive me Will, it is the way of the world and I do share your joy and God shower his blessings on you, Anne and Susanna, it is just that I have brought sad tidings.
William	What is it? Speak?

(turns to Gilbert who says nothing, then to his mother and then to his Father)

John	Your Uncle Edward's valet sent word that his son in law, John Summerville has been taken to the Tower for naming the Queen an heretic and threatening to go to London to kill her.
William	Spare the pagan superstition a death for a birth.
Mary	Do not think such things Will.
William	Summon your strength mother, you know how ruthless our Good Queen has become and her spies need little proof to take their thirty pieces of silver for a life.

Mary	William, you must join me in praying that it not be so.
William	I do mother, I do, but how can God intervene with a monarch who is born of a Father who spurns the true Faith? God spare my child in these times so bad.

Scene 2.

Jonson (recites from the side of the stage, then retires)

> The Shakespeare's home at Henley Street is full to brimming with Will and Anne and their child, and the grandparents John and Mary and William's brother, Gilbert and his surviving sister, Joan. John's business has collapsed and money is hard to come by and Will sees fit to provide a feast.

Exit Jonson

Persons.

John
Mary
William
Anne
Susanna (a baby in bassinet)
Gilbert
Joan
A Soldier

Will enters,

John	What have you there Will?
William	It is a deer kindly donated to the Shakespeare's for a feast by none other than the Queen's lickspittle, Sir Thomas Lucy.
John	That Protestant is not likely to make a feast for those of the old faith like us, lest the fire be lit beneath us.
William	Which is why I thought it only fit that he should pay a penance for his treachery to the true faith.
Mary	But what if you be caught, he's the Queens' man, she's just left his Manor at Charlecot this last week.

William	Well with all the pomp and pageantry they were not quick to notice one deer felled in the shadows and carried off, there's little risk, but let's cook and eat and consume the evidence.
Gilbert	I'll help you take off it's hide.
Joan	And I'll set the fire and a pot boiling while you butcher it.
Mary	And Mother Mary forgive me for pardoning the taking, but this Queen will hold my brother, his wife, their daughter and son-in-law in the Tower so I'll join the feast.
John	Aye, there's nothing we owe those villains.

The light fades on the stage as they set about preparing for the meal.

The stage remains dark, upon it is a bed with William and Anne in it asleep with the bassinet beside it.

Strong Knock upon the Door.

Soldier	Open up, we come upon the Queens' business.
William	(stirs awake) Who calls?
Soldier	We are Sir Thomas Lucy's men and we come for William Shakespeare.
Anne	(stirs) Oh God spare us, you are undone Will.
William	I'll see to it (he rises and goes to the door.)
Soldier	Are you William Shakespeare?
William	I am sir?
Soldier	Then you must come with me under Warrant from Sir Thomas Lucy to answer a charge of poaching his game.
Anne	(Cries out) Oh Will, please be spared.
William	Don't fear Anne, his Lord is mistaken and I will be back by and by.

Scene 3.

The Manor of Sir Thomas Lucy at Charlecot

Persons.

Sir Thomas Lucy

Soldier	
William	
Soldier	Here is the young man who steals from your park m'Lord.
Lucy	Well, what say you, what is your name?
William	Will Shakespeare my Lord.
Lucy	You have been arrested and brought here on my warrant for robbing game from my park, what do you answer?
William	I confess it is true my Lord but though I cannot proffer an excuse I can proffer an explanation.
Lucy	What explanation can you provide that will exonerate you from this offence young man?
William	Sir, I do not claim exoneration.
Lucy	Well what purpose is there in your words, let me cut them short and commit you to prison while I, as the Queens' justice decide whether to have you hanged.
William	M'Lord before you send me away I pray hear me, you are by reputation a God fearing man and you will remember Christ's teaching from the Sermon on the Mount in Matthew Chapter 5, Verse 42 Jesus said, "Give him that asketh thee, and from him that would borrow from you turn not away."
Lucy	It serves you well that you recall the Gospel young Shakespeare but I do not remember you asking for my deer.
William	No My Lord I confess that is true.
Lucy	And let me quote some scripture to you in return, Chapter 5 of Matthew , Verse 25 "Agree with thine adversary quickly, whiles thy art in the way with him; lest at any time thy adversary deliver thee to the Judge, and the Judge deliver thee to the Officer and thou be cast into prison." Now that being so do you agree with the charge.
William	I do so agree My Lord.
Lucy	I know of your family young Shakespeare, your Father though mistaken in his beliefs is a good man, our local chief alderman and

	now it is known to me he has fallen on hard times.
William	That is true sir.
Lucy	And what account do you make of yourself apart from poaching?
William	I am apprenticed to my father as a glover, lest I was until my new wife delivered me of a child early this year.
Lucy	So you are a husband and a father.
William	Aye, all of those sir.
Lucy	And how did you come by your learning of the Bible, did you read the Latin?
William	Yes sir I was at the Grammar School until I was fourteen.
Lucy	And your studies ended with your apprenticeship did you want to study at university?
William	It was my dream My Lord but my family needed income.
Lucy	You know I can have you hanged for stealing?
William	I do sir.
Lucy	I cannot on your confession let you free young man and so I will commit you to prison, but it will not be for long and you will not hang.
William	Thank you My Lord.
Lucy	But when you are released, which shall be at my pleasure, you are to take your affairs hence from Stratford and not return for a year, and if you do, be warned that I might change my mind. Soldier take him to the prison and send word to the Borough Clerk so that young Shakespeare's friends take a lesson.
Soldier	(Placing his hand on William's shoulder) Come on son, I hope you are not scared of rats and dark dank stone. (Leads William off)

Scene 4.

Persons.

John
Mary
Anne
(Susanna the babe)
Gilbert
Joan

Enter William

Anne	Oh thank God it's Will, you are returned.
William	I promised by and by and it was only a week; not too much for a good feast!
John	What did befall you?
William	I've written a ballad for my Lord Lucy which he would not care for much, but although he threw me in his dungeon for a spell he spared my neck.
Mary	Oh Will, thank God you are back and do not jest about hanging.
William	What, do not leave me dangling.
John	No Will this is too solemn a subject, we are grateful to the Lord for your return but it did not go so well for your uncle, your cousin and their wives.
William	Oh Lord, what has befallen them.
Mary	Poor John Summerville took his own life, but for the others, his wife, my brother Edward and their wives, though no fault be found in them of plotting against the Queen she had them one and all hanged, drawn and quartered at the meat market at Smithfield.
Anne	It is too monstrous to comprehend yet this is the work of our Royal line of Tudor.
John	Who can comprehend the madness that flows from a king rampant with lust and madness who disowns his religion, kills his wives, and has a child who acting out the madness imprisons her own sister, Queen Mary and threatens her with the noose; this then is the good Queen Bess.

Mary	First she takes my husband away and now she kills my family. (Mary breaks down weeping)
William	Oh no, mother, forgive me to make light of this monstrous peril.
Mary	And now you have been locked away and by one of her most trusted henchman, Lucy. You must think about your life, if not for my sake for that of Anne, Susanna your Father, Gilbert and Joan.
William	(Comforting his mother) We will triumph through this mother.
John	What do you mean Will?
William	Father, you have escaped the Tower, and I have escaped Sir Thomas Lucy but the ice is thin and the lake is cold and deep. He has commanded me to be banished from the borough for a year and if I stay more tragedy could follow.
Mary	Well you must go, and go in haste for I could not bear to lose more of those I love.
Anne	What is this Will, what banishment?
William	I confessed the theft of the deer to Sir Thomas, he looked into my eyes and I to his and I saw that the truth was the proper way and yet in that I am confirmed a thief in his eyes; but there was some mercy that I now do apprehend the more with this terrible news of the Ardens.
Anne	And what mercy is that?
William	That if I leave I will not be hanged, and there is the promise of my return if I stay fast a year away.
Gilbert	Where will you go Will and what about Anne and Susanna?
John	They will be safe with us but Will you must take up your teaching that was promised with the Houghtons.
William	I will see Master Cottam and make it firm and do not fret Anne for my life is spared, but forgetting my own travail will be nothing compared to the pain and the horror of the Ardens.
Mary	Let us preserve what remains.

John	I have a little money to help you and you can send us missives which your brother or Anne can read to us.
William	I am sorry Anne.
Anne	Will, I cannot love a dead man, so go tomorrow if you can, and live for Susanna and me; we will be safe here.

ACT 5

Jonson (recites from the side of the stage, then retires)

The Fifth Act.   And then the justice,
In fair round belly with good capon lin'd,
With eyes severe and beard of formal cut,
Full of wise saws and modern instances;
And so he plays his part.

This scene finds us 200 miles away at Houghton
Tower at the Houghton Estate Lancashire.

Exit Jonson

Scene 1.

Persons.
John Cottam
Alexander Houghton
William
(in Sir Alexander's library awaiting him)

Cottam	Will, Sir Alexander's family themselves are in the Lord Burghley's lists of sympathisers with the Old Faith as are your family and the Ardens, so you can be candid with him about your mother's family, your Father's arrest and your recent dealings with Sir Thomas Lucy.
William	I am grateful for your recommendation as a tutor, however I must confess to him no experience in teaching.
Cottam	You have acted some in the Guildhall at Stratford so there's for the drama and the

	rest will be as you had with me at the petty and Kings School in Stratford.
William	Will I be assisted by an usher to help with the younger pupils?
Cottam	Sir Alexander will let us know. Here you are privileged because although our good Queen has ordered the burning of books, Sir Alexander has retained a secret repository of the books you studied. You will be able to teach the older pupils Latin.
William	What indelible memories I have of William Lily's Short Introduction of Grammar; although I may not be as strict a Master as when I was taught with the proscription against speaking of English.
Cottam	But here you will be able to read anthologies of Latin sayings and Aesop's Fables; you will have the joy of your favourite plays of Terence and Plautus and with your recent forays into the stage you can direct the pupils to act scenes from the Latin plays.

(Enter Sir Alexander)

Alexander	Welcome John, and welcome young man, you have come highly commended by my good friend Cottam, your old Master I believe.
William	Thankyou Sir Alexander.
Alexander	Let us make a bond between ourselves here and now that some matters require the utmost secrecy. You know there is talk of this mad Queen who tried her half sister Mary Queen of Scots for treason now looking for necks afresh to stretch to her ways?
Cottam	It is a deadly duel between the Crown and the Church. When we go to confessional in secret we are asked to confess our allegiance.

Alexander	And our family has by Royal command been asked to declare the opposite allegiance against the Roman Church to her Majesty.
William	And sir there are deadly penalties for the wrong utterances.
Alexander	I know of the fate which has befallen your mother's family. In the midst of this madness we have retained here in Houghton Castle a full ecclesiastical library so that our children might be taught in secret, the matters we took at ease. Have you any thoughts?
William	I have the model of my own education at the Kings School at Stratford. I believe I will have access to Virgil, Plato, Socrates, Seneca, Plautus, Euripides and Ovid.
Alexander	Indeed you and your students can indulge in books, both classical and modern which we have preserved away from the barbarism of the Queen and her spies.
William	I will begin as we did with the traditional learning then attempt to improve their command with translation from Latin into English and back. With the library the pupils will have models of style, and manuals of composition. I would like to teach the ancient rules of rhetoric and they would compose formal epistles, orations, and declamations. If it is not presumptuous I wish to teach the newer rules of writing and composition. Finally, Sir, my great love is the theatre and so there will be plays as you might deem appropriate.
Cottam	He is well versed in all these Sir Alexander, a brilliant student who was destined for University but for the calamity of his father's bankruptcy.
Alexander	Cambridge's loss is then our gain, and William, let me welcome you as our new Master, but for safety you might alter your name a little on any local records, you may

	be Will Shakeshafte, a clerk in my service and nothing more as concerns the village.
William	Yes sir, a fine synonym, Shakeshafte, it fits well.
Alexander	And from my information you would be wise to use that when travelling to and from Stratford to see your wife and child, at least for the present.
William	I have had a tryst with Sir Thomas Lucy.
Alexander	He, like the good Lord Burghley is a man to be wary of, for he has the close confidence of our Queen and follows her ways.
Cottam	And those ways, alas!
William	She is a beggar on horseback, the horse is unreined, though she be reigning and they gallop with us all tied to the stirrups.
Alexander	Well put young Shakeshafte (laughing)

Scene 2.

Jonson (recites from the side of the stage, then retires)

> Our beloved William Shakespeare or Shakeshafte returns many times quietly to Stratford and we find him back there using his own name in 1587, now the proud father of three children, Susanna and the twins Judith and Hamnet delivered by Anne in 1585.

Exit Jonson

Persons.

Anne
William
James Burbage

Enter William and James to the kitchen at Henley Street where Anne is sitting at the table, reading.

William	What reading takes your fancy Anne?
Anne	Hello Will, I have the poem Venus and Adonis you wrote and I am very taken with it, it is brilliant, oh I am sorry, (noticing James behind Will) hello James, what brings you up from London?
James	I am back to see to business Anne, to visit Will's father and commiserate with him and to assist where ever I can.
Anne	It has been wonderful to have my husband back from the exile imposed by Sir Thomas what proposal do you bring James, not more exile I trust?
James	You know I have my playhouse at Shoreditch in London and I might have found work for Will.
Anne	We have need of work, one of us, for times are quite hard for our family and Will has had to travel because of the problem with Sir Thomas Lucy.
James	I have talked with my son Richard and he is busy with acting and we both would like Will to join us and help us with some new plays.
Anne	And what can the theatre offer us?
James	Well I will come to that soon Anne but chance has struck with good fortune I hope. Do you know the Players are in Stratford this weekend to perform The Troublesome Reign of King John?
Anne	Yes Will told me as much but of greater interest to me is to be amused by Tarleton, it is said even in these times he can make us laugh.
James	Oh indeed he can, he is uproarious, and can utter words that would send most of us to the Tower, and he does so, even in the presence of her Majesty.
William	James has brought us tickets and more!

Anne	More of what?
James	More exile I am afraid but there is money to be made and with Will's father discharged from the council and suffering the fate of a bankrupt the family cannot survive on Will's income as a teacher.
William	An opportunity has come Anne which I wish to seize with both hands. The Company are to perform in the Guildhall but their principal actor William Nell has been killed.
Anne	What is this, what has happened?
James	On their way to Stratford the company was hostelled at the White Heart and their principal actor, Nell has come to blows with another of the company John Towne who knifed him in defence and thereby slew him.
William	Towne has been imprisoned for murder.
Anne	What means this to us?
James	Towne has been replaced but the lead has no replacement; but for Will; because of my old position as Head of the Earl of Leicester's Players, I have convinced my old friend who runs the troupe that Will could play his part.
William	I know the lines and can perform the part, and it will pay handsomely.
Anne	And what then, should you succeed, will you travel on with these players?
William	That is my hope dear Anne.
Anne	Do not these players roam about the countryside pushing the Queens' message against our Church?
James	Aye indeed, one of the lines goes. "If King John be crowned, then nore pope, nor spain nor france shall do them wrong." Remember though, the wind gathers in the

	Queens' sails with the people because of the threat from Spain. These are patriotic times.
William	I know that will not sit well with our faithful Anne, but it is a stepping stone for us, and public religion as we know is a flighty thing, I do not care what public utterance is made, especially through the mouth of a player.
Anne	Well, if that is what you want Will, and it can profit the family you know I will remain steadfast.
William	I promise you this, my beloved, when the actors speak my lines between, within and underneath I'll tell the truth, though outwardly we know it can cost a life.
Anne	And Will, this family has paid enough and yours is not for sale.
James	If all goes well Anne, when Will gets to London he can join us in our theatre at Shoreditch but it must be understood that if it unfolds to be, then William may be further away.
Anne	(Laughing) Will often calls me a hater, but he knows I love him. It is the Queen I hate and her loathsome retinue. I am a country woman, well disposed and trusting of my boyish spouse and should he prosper then all of us will prosper, such is his loyalty to us, so you must do whatever you can Will, there is nothing here in Stratford.
William	My dearest Anne, you have saved my life.
Anne	Enough praise Will, you go and save all our lives, and spare seats for me and your parents at the performance and watch my face when you utter those anti-papist lines.
William	I dare not look at any face when that time comes.
James	It is done then, thank you for your blessing Anne.

Anne   (Aside to James) Thanks to you James, you are a true friend to us all and don't think me a simple country wife, I was happy to live my life as a maid until Will gave his love to me. You must know James, there will never be another Will Shakespeare, I know that, even though he has only guessed it.

Scene 3.

Jonson (recites from the side of the stage, then retires)

    William is only 23 years old, he has been off travelling and acting with the Players Company, until they arrive in London and then ....

Persons.

William
Richard Burbage
James Burbage
Henry Condell

James   Welcome to London William, how good to see you.

William   James, I cannot thank you enough, we have travelled as far as Edinburgh playing the Queens' plays.

James   You know my son Richard, do you remember him from Stratford.

William   Aye I do, how goes it Richard?

Richard   Good Will, welcome to London, have you slipped the Queens' Players.

William   I have given them good service and they have one of their own retinue to happily play the lead, so I am free of that politic.

Richard   I have heard you have some plays in your sack.

William   Has your father been giving me too much praise, I fear it might be so!

Richard	Not at all, not at all, but the time is right for new material, the stage is alive and money is to be made, we need another Marlowe or Jonson.
William	I might not be of that order but I do have some plays. I have rewritten The Tragical History of King Lear and Richard the Third which we did with the Queens Company but I have continued to polish them.
James	Is there more?
William	Well, James, I have embarked upon some history plays based on material from Holinshed's The Chronicles of England, Scotland and Ireland.
Richard	We need something to entertain the groundlings and we can worry about the historians once we have them in the theatre, what have you that would amuse our crowds?
William	Well I have also rewritten The Historie of Error which was performed at Hampton Court a few years back, but I have taken little from that which was not already stolen from Plautus' Menaechmi.
Richard	Father and I know little of Plautus and I for one have not heard of The Historie of Error so can you describe your Comedy of Errors.
William	Well in essence it is a farce.
James	Oh excellent, a comedy.
William	Yes of sorts James, but the situations are stranger still. In Menaechmi, Plautus has a man in search of his long-lost twin brother and in that encounters his twins' wife, his mistress, and his father and they mistake the one for the other. I have gone a step onwards by giving the brothers both called Antipholus a servant both called Dromio who themselves are long-separated twins.
Richard	This is what we want, tell us more.

William	I start the play with a serious opening, a scene with the twin's father, Aegeon, who has arrived at Ephesus from Syracuse in search of them. He is arrested and I have the Duke of Ephesus, Solinus, saying , "It hath in solemn synods been decreed, both by the Syracusans and ourselves, to admit no traffic to our adverse towns," and it continues "If any Syracusan born come to the bay of Ephesus, he dies."
James	Ah, you have used the story of Apollonius of Tyre as your inspiration for this beginning.
William	That is right, and unless he finds someone to redeem him he is to die. We then proceed to a scene in which Antipholus of Ephesus' wife, Adriana, bars him from his own house. It turns out that she is at that time entertaining his brother. For this I gathered the idea from another play by Plautus, Amphitruo.
Richard	How do you picture it being staged, Will?
William	I have used the three 'houses' — the Phoenix, the Porcupine, and the Priory — represented by doors and signs on stage.
James	And how do you round it all up?
William	The family are separated initially in a shipwreck . From this they survive but all the twins are separated one from the other and the Mother from the Father. So we have Aegeon, the father in Ephesus, Amelia the mother in Syracuse, the two twins separated become Antipholous of Syracuse, and Antipholous of Ephesus and the two servants Dromio of Syracuse and Dromio of Ephesus. The tragedy is that the Syracusan Antipholous does not redeem his own father. The mother, Amelia fearing all her family were lost has become a nun, and eventually an Abbess of Syracuse. It is she, who comes to the sad situation and declares "speak old Aegeon, if thou be'st the man that had'st a wife once called Amelia."
Richard	Well done, so all is saved after much calamitous hilarity and pathos. It is superb Will and we will rehearse it at once.

Scene 4.

Jonson (recites from the side of the stage, then retires)

It is now 1592 and the theatre at Blackfriars has prospered with performances of Two Gentlemen of Verona, Love's Labour's Lost, Henry VI, Richard III , Titus Andronicus and Taming of the Shrew. Will at 28 has become one of 16 shareholders with the Burbages and others in the Theatre. He is the most famous playwright in all of England! This scene finds itself at the Green Dragon Inn, Bishopsgate.

Exit Jonson

Persons.
Christopher Marlowe
Richard Burbage
William Shakespeare

William	Where else can a man buy his friends drinks called a left leg?
Marlow	Or Dragon's brew, there's something to imbibe to put power up your spout.
Burbage	You two are not just champions of the theatre but drinking champions of Bishopsgate.
William	It is a world within the world here Richard, a stroll to Shoreditch brings the entertainment of bear bating, skittle alleys, gambling dens and better still barmaids who bear their breasts and when a man can endure no more vice, he can pay his penance back at St. Helen's in Bishopsgate.
Marlow	And my religiosity has been amply repaid with the adulation of my adoring audience.
Burbage	You Cambridge men are all the same, you did it on your own didn't you Kit?
Marlow	Forgive me I sometimes forget to be humble. Where would my Tamberlaine be without the great Edward Alleyn.
William	You have been kind to him Kit, buying him fame enough to build his school, Dulwich College.

Marlow	In vino veritas, let me confess to my two closest allies, without the like of your Richard Burbage, and Augustine Phillips, Kit Beaston, Henry Condell, Will Kemp, Thomas Pope, Will Slye and Edward Alleyn my plays would have lain on the floor of the bar.
William	And my truth is Kit that without you having found the finest players alive and Fernando Stanley paying for production, my first plays Titus Andronicus, Henry 6 and so on would have never survived, and let me not forget Richard and his good father James making a gift to me of the Theatre for the performances. I am forever in debt to you both.
Marlow	The greatest miracle is that we have been good enough to survive the reformist zeal of our Queen by keeping her too amused to hang us.
Burbage	Is it so bad, have we risked so much?
Marlow	I cannot speak for your lives gentlemen, but mine hangs slenderly at the moment, ah, but what feeds me will destroy me.
William	Don't speak that way Kit, you are at the height of your powers.
Marlow	Alas, not just on paper but in the wide open spaces as well my friend.
Burbage	What are you babbling about in this mournful way Marlowe.
Marlow	The Queen has spies even in Holland where I was wont to mention that those who love not tobacco and boys are fools; Protestants are hypocritical asses; Jesus was a bastard, the Virgin Mary was a whore and John the evangelist Christ's bedfellow.
Burbage	If you said a mite of that here Kit we would be at your funeral the next day.
Marlow	And so you will be Richard for it is as though my folly were committed here because that is what the Queens' spying dog Robert Poley has reported me as saying. He was with me in Holland.
William	Surely there is a mistake here Kit, you are not so incautious!

Marlow	Well, I can't remember those particular lines Will, but I do recall talking about going over to the Catholic side and counterfeiting coin of the Realm to take with me before joining the enemy.
Burbage	But Kit why would you put so much at risk? You must be raking money in from the Rose Theatre, why counterfeit more? You know the mad Queen has just executed two printers for sedition?
Marlow	If I knew why it is, that I am as I am, then the riddle of myself would be solved but I have been ordered back here to London by her Majesty's inquisitors and I am to make my reckoning with them this very evening. Let me buy us all a left leg to celebrate and with the money you two are making with Henry 6 Part 3 you can pay the bill.
William	Of course we can do that and more. We are getting hundreds in the galleries and a half a thousand groundlings in the pit every show.
Marlowe	You must pay for that because you are getting better numbers than my Jew of Malta, so you must be giving free beer because my play is by far the better.
Burbage	Let's not descend to jealous banter lest we sound like that sad dead competitor, Robert Greene who from his grave has his publisher put his spite about.
Marlowe	What new spite is this?
William	Oh he lambasts us all Kit, exhorting you to stop writing and calling me a Johannes Factotum, an upstart crow.
Marlowe	Who cares what he says, (raises his glass in toast) here's to the Queen, may she rot in hell. I must be off to meet her satyrs and let Greene stay green with his envy for all eternity.

Marlowe stumbles out.

Burbage	I fear for Marlowe, and the way he speaks he knows what awaits him.
William	I fear so; I have felt the sword of authority right up to the tang as it slashed at my

family and it has made me careful when I take my way, each trifle under truest bars to thrust.

Scene 5.
Jonson (recites from the side of the stage, then retires)

It is only the next day and this scene finds William at the Theatre with the company of actors who are his close friends and about to rehearse for the night's performance.

Exit Jonson

Persons.
Richard Burbage
Henry Condell
Will Slye
Augustin Phillips
William Shakespeare
John Heminges
(All actors)

Burbage	Last night Will and I were with him and now he's dead.
Condell	The story that is about, is that it was a quarrel over a debt, that Kit Marlowe beat Ingram Frizzard over the head with the base of his dagger, and Frizzard in defence took it off him and stabbed him through the right eye.
William	It is true I am afraid at least the report of his death. I heard the story at the Black Bull. Kit was lured from the Watergate on the Thames to Elena Bull's house Deptford
Phillips	The same Elena Bull who is cousin to the Queen's torturer Frances Walsingham.
William	The same, and at the house his company was none other than the scoundrel Nicholas Skyres who plotted with his ilk to destroy

	Mary Queen of Scots, also Robert Pooley and Ingram Frizzard.
Burbage	Each one a spy for the Queen.
Slye	All they would need is to see his latest play Edward the Second about a corrupt ruler and a fawning court .
William	No! Kit had written his own death warrant with his visit to Holland; having lured him back, these scoundrels conspire to call his murder a drunken brawl over the moneys owing at the Inn. The truth is not to understand a man's verses can kill a man more dead than a great reckoning in a little room.
Burbage	In this England, life is only as valuable as the Queen allows.
Phillips	Let us press on with our rehearsal, the Puritans want to close the playhouses and with the plague on London's doorstep they will have all the reason they need.
William	We've talked of this before, make our money while we can and you all should have put some aside.
Phillips	None of us can complain.
William	More than the money, we should all plan what to do when that time comes because Phillips is right, the theatres will close and for how long we cannot know but let us pledge to reunite when this cloud passes.
Burbage	What of your plans Will, back to Stratford?
William	That and more Richard, I want to write a book of sonnets. Have you heard of John Dee.
Burbage	I have indeed, the astronomer.
William	He is that and more, but he is a mystic as well and a scryer, a man who studies the crystal spheres and he has written of his discourse with the spirits in his Mysteriorum Liber Primus.
Phillips	He is a man of superstition and science, is that a contradiction?
William	Well perhaps so, you know my faith; but I have had an epiphany of sorts.
Burbage	What are you telling us Will?
William	It was not scrying, it was not alchemy but I best explain it as an epiphany, I have

	written it up in a Sonnet and when there is no call for plays I will write some more.
Slye	What interest do you have in John Dee?
William	I have slender regard for much of his astrology but I confess an interest with his belief in numbers.
Phillips	And what of these numbers?
William	Well things have their numbers, a man has seven ages, a deck of cards has four suits, and sometimes unless you know the right numbers things have no meaning.
Burbage	Tell us more?
William	I will tell you this, I will write 154 sonnets, divide it by 7 the seven ages a man lives.
Slye	That gives us 22.
William	Now each 22 fulfils part of the seven ages, and then you take them all like cards and throw them in the air and when they land you renumber them all, except Sonnet 33.
Slye	It is your riddle Will?
William	That it is, Will, that it is, but the rest of me is an open book for any stage but my faith is enshrined in the number 33 as for the rest, even the Queens' spies will not follow my true thoughts.
Heminges	We all feel devastated by the loss of Kit Marlow Will; it is the best of times for some of us and the worst of times for others.
William	I must confess John that I am torn as are we all. My own family has been ravaged by the Queens' madness and yet our company continues to prosper with her support.
Burbage	It does not profit our families to be martyrs to her madness.
William	No, but loyalties are torn and my cousin some removed, Robert Southwell is in hiding from the Queen's inquisitors but has dedicated his last book called St. Peter's Complaint and Saint Mary Magdalens Funeral Tears with Sundry Other Selected and Decent Poems with the words To my worthy good cousin, Master WS."
Heminges	And who might Master WS be Will?
William	A study of his genealogy will bring you to my door. My cousin both honours and abjures me saying "worthy poets by

	abusing their talents and by making the
	follys and feignings of love the subject of
	their base endeavours, have so discredited
	this faculty that a poet, a lover and a lyer
	are but three words of one signification."
Slye	Does he want your head in the noose and
	your children orphans?
William	No, but he goads me about my faith, my
	calling, my profession and he supports his
	argument with the risk of his life, it is not to
	be discounted, this gesture.
Burbage	But you must decide Will whether to use
	your words to deliver you life or your life to
	deliver your words.
William	I have concluded as much Richard and that
	is my course but I will say what I can in my
	sonnets and answer my cousin's call to
	praise that which should be praised in
	them.
Burbage	Let our hearts lighten some and back to
	rehearsal for we have our dates confirmed
	and the audiences are waiting.

ACT 6

Scene 1.

Enter Jonson

    The sixth age shifts
  Into the lean and slipper'd pantaloon,
   With spectacles on nose and pouch on side,
  His youthful hose, well saved, a world too wide,
For his shrunk shank;
   His big manly voice turning towards childish treble
pipes
   And whistles in his sound.
        ...but not quite yet...
        William is only 32 and this scene finds our
        leading man in Kent early august 1596 with
        the players who now formed the
        Chamberlains men.
        William had written Romeo and Juliet,
        another masterpiece which now featured in
        their performances.

Exit Jonson.

Persons
Henry Condell
William Shakespeare
Richard Burbage
A Messenger

(The three actors enter the stage from the stage as it were, in costume having just finished a performance of Romeo and Juliet)

Burbage	The crowd are in tears.
Condell	It caught me tonight, when Romeo died, I felt that I was dying.
William	It is only a play Henry.

(Knocking on the door, messenger enters in haste)

Burbage	What news young fellow you look as though you were in the front row of our play.
Messenger	No sire, I have ridden hard and my mind has been in turmoil with news for Master Shakespeare.
William	My heart is pounding, I know this is grave, tell me what brings you in such haste this late hour?
Messenger	Be you Master William Shakespeare of Stratford?
William	That I am now tell me?
Messenger	Sir, is it fit to speak of the most damned matters concerning your family in company?
William	Yes, speak, these are my friends.
Messenger	Sir, I bring black news from Mrs. Shakespeare that you should come at once to Stratford.
William	What has happened?
Messenger	Sir, I am sorry to tell you that your son, Hamnet has gone to heaven.
William	No, tell me this is not true.
Messenger	It be true sir, I would not carry such a calumny otherwise.
William	How is he dead?

Messenger	Mrs. Shakespeare said to tell you he took ill and was wracked with rigors then dropped into a sleep from which he did not wake.
William	Holy Mother of God spare me this news. When did he die?
Messenger	On 11ᵗʰ August sir.
William	He was 11 years old, oh no, I cannot bear it.
Burbage	Will, it is 13ᵗʰ August now, go at once, I will ride with you to keep you awake lest he be interred before you see his face.
Condell	I will arrange horses at once, William my heart aches for you.
William	The world is cruel and bends my mind out of all proportion, what am I to do? What am I to do? I cannot live in this world, but I must go, quick find the horses, where is my cloak?
Burbage	Come Will, even if we ride all night I will see you back to Stratford.

Scene 2.

At the Shakespeare's home at Henley Street the next day.

Persons
John Shakespeare
Mary Shakespeare
Gilbert Shakespeare
Anne Shakespeare
Richard Burbage

Enter William and Burbage; William's wife, brother and his parents sit in silence with a small white coffin upon a stand.

Anne	(Weeping) Oh Will, Richard thank God you have come.
William	What has happened to our beautiful son, I should have been here.
John	Will, he was baptized in the faith and he is at rest in the arms of our Lord Jesus.
William	Oh, Father, what misery to endure to lose my son when I still have life?

John	Will, this is what our faith is for, to endure what life delivers.
William	How did he die?
Mary	This time last week Will he was cock-a-hoop, leaping around and happy and then he began to cough and suddenly there were birthmarks all about his arms.
Anne	He cried and told us that his head was hurting, so we put him to bed and called the doctor.
John	The good doctor came at once, but Hamnet by then was lapsed into sleep, a fever raged upon his brow and nothing would wake him.
William	Was it the plague?
Mary	The doctor said it was not, but a malady that could not be cured. He tried to rouse him and administered every cure he could find in his kit, but Hamnet stiffened, moaned and then the doctor told us to call the Priest.
William	Did you have a Priest of our Faith.
John	Aye, I saw to that , good Father Frith came and gave him the Last Rites and he died in his mother's arms.
William	And Judith and Susanna, where are they?
Anne	They have gone with a nurse to my brother at Shottery.
William	Are they well?
John	Yes Will, they are, they are, it is an affliction that visited only upon Hamnet, took his young life and went.
William	Is he lying there, is the coffin sealed (moves over to the coffin)
Mary	Go easily Will, he lies within, dressed in his Kings' School clothing, he loved his school.
William	(Opens the lid on the coffin) Oh my son, my beautiful son, There you lie, serene, It is still you, but the quickness has flown Oh, what misery to look upon one so young ….It is like yesterday when you were plucked Like a perfect saint from your mother's womb You opened your eyes and looked at me

And there I saw my life, my reason
The meaning behind all my pretence and
play acting
There delivered from my loving wife
My son, my son, my son
And what promise, in this new being
Who renewed his mother and father
With every look, and laugh and smile
To come to this! Lying like wax
The spirit gone, and with it my heart,
My life, my love, my future.
(William collapses weeping)

Scene 3.

Enter Jonson.

William remains at Stratford after the
funeral of his only son. It is six weeks after
the burial and the Shakespeare's house at
Henley Street is full.

Exit Jonson.

Persons.
John Shakespeare
Mary Shakespeare
William
Anne

William	I have been away too long and too much.
Mary	Son, do not chide yourself, your hard work has done much for your family.
William	How can I forgive myself for being away on the stage while my son lay dying?
Anne	Don't talk that way Will, you know better, it happened so quickly you could have been in Snitterfield toiling in the fields and been just as absent. No-one is to blame, all of us share the grief and we share it together.
William	I thank God for your love and wisdom Anne but you know I am restless and always caught up in action, and I mean to put things to rights.

John	What do you mean Will, there is nothing more you can do for us you have been so kind already, do not do more, it will shame me for my own business failings.
William	No father, my intention is never to suggest any shortcoming in you. You and mother have played my role and I can never thank you enough for caring for Anne and the children in your home. I mean to make amends and have bought the old house next to the Kings School. It has five gables and is quite grand. It is close by for you and mother to visit and we in return, but it will mean you can have your home back to yourselves.
Mary	But we have loved having Anne and the children here, it has been a blessing and a joy.
John	And Will, that place is grand but it has been derelict for some while and will need repair.
William	That it will father, but the Burbages were builders and Richard has procured all the workmen we need to restore its grandeur. If it is alright with you and mother we will stay awhile until the renovations are complete.
John	If it is alright, of course it is alright, you can stay forever son and indeed I cannot see your mother letting any of you go.
Mary	I am not so fond John to deny Anne her own house, she is the most beautiful daughter-in-law but let her have her own home and let Will carry her over the threshold when it be done.
John	Well that is it then, your mother has spoken and you know Will she is usually right.
Mary	Of course I am right and a happy home it shall be Will.
Anne	Thank you Will, it has a lovely garden and we will be happy there.
William	It is the very least I could do, but I mean to set another thing right.
John	What now?
William	Well Father, you have suffered much and now that you are older I want you to have

	more than comfort, I want you to have the rank you and mother deserve.
John	What is this?
William	Do you remember when you were Chief Alderman and proposed to apply for a Coat of Arms?
John	Oh, pomp and pageant, yes, look Will I've come to accept things as they are and it was my vanity, remember Ecclesiastes? Since then I've been thrown off the council and been bankrupted.
William	Look Father, it is a vain bubble, but I have applied for Letters Patent, why not rejoin the past and what harm can it do?
John	Well what have you done?
William	I have applied to the College of Arms in London and having proved your lineage and the aristocratic line of my mother, they have seen fit to grant you Letters Patent for a Coat of Arms with the motto, Non Sanz Droit.
John	Well it sounds good but what does it mean?
William	Not without right.
John	Not without right eh? Well that sounds good enough for me, thank you Will, you make me proud.
Mary	And what will be on the coat of Arms Will?
William	An Eagle clasping a spear.
Mary	Thank you Will. (William embraces his father)
Anne	(Aside to Mary) Oh mother forgive me, but we must humour Will he suffers so for Hamnet that I fear for his mind. If he looked at this with reason he would see the sadness of buying a Coat of Arms; he has a title, but no son to inherit it. (she weeps)
Mary	(Comforting her) He needs to be doing something, it stops him mourning so keep him busy Anne, just keep him busy and you put your mind on happy things to ease this dreadful pain.

Scene 4
Enter Jonson.

It is summer of 1597 and the theatres were closed again for sedition but William is back in London busying himself with poetry and other pursuits.

Exit Jonson

Persons.
William
Richard Burbage

William   My art is tongue-tied by authority, and I have fallen behind with city taxes. I am too well known living near St. Helens, I fear I must leave Bishopsgate.

Burbage   I can help you find a place at Southwark but how pressing are your concerns?

William   I am in debt to William Waite and he has sought sureties of the peace against me proclaiming fear of death or mutilation of limbs by me. It is all a lie except that I owe him money but he means to put me in harms' way.

Burbage   Then go south of the river, it is rough but you know your way around and no-one will find you there unless you want them to; you can busy yourself with your poetry, or take in some bear baiting or dog fighting.

William   Thanks Richard, I do not know my own mind. It is a hell of a time for me at the moment and though I have provided for Anne and the children and I have property, money is in short supply and my health is suffering.

Burbage   Then I will settle it for you Will, come with me to Southwark and we will move you swiftly and then I will take you to Dr. Foreman to remedy your ills.

(They leave, lights fade on the stage)

Scene 5.

Enter Jonson.

Will has moved to Southwark and now
waits upon Dr. Foreman

Exit Jonson

Persons.
William
Dr. Foreman
Emilia Lanier

(William is waiting upon the doctor in an ante room with
Emilia waiting also.)

William	Is the doctor your physician?
Emilia	(Shyly) He is sir, is he not yours as well?
William	I come on the recommendation of a friend.
Emilia	You have come to a good man sir, not only learned in medicine but also astrology.
William	I do not take my judgment from the stars.
Emilia	Then what guides you good sir?
William	The eyes.
Emilia	Indeed, whose eyes?
William	The eyes into which I look (he gazes at her)
Emilia	And what do you see in my eyes?
William	From thine eyes my knowledge I derive, And from the constant stars in them I read such art, As truth and beauty shall together thrive.
Emilia	That is beautiful, do you read poetry?
William	I read it and I write it.
Emilia	And who wrote those lines?
William	Those lines are mine, from me to you.
Emilia	But you do not know me?
William	I wish that I could?
Emilia	Oh sir, you have come here with a malady and you start wooing a stranger.
William	Perhaps I have come here to meet my lady rather than arriving with a malady.
Emilia	You are quick of thought sir, will you tell me your name.
William	I am William Shakespeare.
Emilia	Then I know who you are, you are famous sir.

William	Am I famous enough to ask you your own name?
Emilia	My name is Emilia.
William	Is my fame mighty enough to permit me to ask if I might meet you some time outside the doctor's waiting room?
Emilia	You are most forward sir, but gentle with it, if your health will allow, you might come tonight to the Salon near the Mermaid and watch me play the clavichord, I will be performing tonight.
William	At what hour and I will be there?
Emilia	At six tonight.

(Enter Dr. Foreman)

Foreman	(turning to Will) Good afternoon Sir, are you Richard's friend?
William	Yes indeed doctor, William Shakespeare.
Foreman	I know your name Mr. Shakespeare I will be pleased to be of service to you, would you kindly wait while I see Miss Lanier?
William	I will wait upon her forever if it be required.
Foreman	No sir, it will not be forever but a little time, if you please (turning) now Miss Lanier will you come in.

Dr. Foreman leads Emilia into his consulting room.

Scene 6.

Enter Jonson

That night, true to his word, indeed his word had little to do with it, nothing would have impeded our playwright being at the Salon at Lothbury near the Mermaid Inn.

Exit Jonson

Persons.
Emilia Lanier
William
A small appreciative audience

(The audience small in number but including William, who sits, back to the audience, while Emilia Lanier finishes her clavichord piece, she bows and makes to leave the instrument towards the right of the stage and William follows, detaining her)

Emilia	Oh you've come; and was it to your liking?
William	I envy those jacks that nimble leap, To kiss the tender inward of thy hand.
Emilia	More poetry from Mr. Shakespeare, you need not be jealous of the keys (putting her hand forward), you may kiss my hand.
William	(Taking her hand tenderly and kissing it) Emilia, may I tell you that you are beautiful and that in the instant I saw your dark eyes I was changed forever?
Emilia	You do not need my permission to declare yourself so, but it is at your risk sir, for I am married to another man.
William	And I dear Emilia, am alike married and so we are alike.
Emilia	Alike is not enough dear Mr. Shakespeare.
William	Will you join me at the Mermaid for some ale and food?
Emilia	You are persistent against all odds.
William	With you I don't know when to stop.
Emilia	I'll spare your misery and join you, it would be uncharitable not to assist a man in such distress, and yet I thought the doctor would cure you.
William	I fear I have a complaint that is beyond medicine.
Emilia	I trust that I am not the source of your present discomfiture Mr. Shakespeare.
William	It is Will, if I may, Emilia.
Emilia	Will it is, and will in overplus when it comes to pursuing a lady.
William	Not any lady Emilia, just you.

They leave together.
(the light fades on the stage and the scenery is replaced with a four post bed in which, when the light returns lie our two lovers)

Emilia	Will you make me a lady William?

William	Dear Emilia I will give you everything I own but we both are married and have last night broken our bed vows.
Emilia	My husband has gone and I know not if he will return.
William	My wife waits upon me at Stratford and I am foresworn not to divorce, it cannot be.
Emilia	Then you have used me sir, as the Lord Chamberlain Hunsden has done, putting me with child and then marrying me to a minstrel in his keep. The same minstrel who faithless, in turn, left me alone with my child.
William	I will not leave you alone nor ever see you go without Emilia, but I cannot give you what my faith will not permit.
Emilia	Last night you gave me more than your faith would permit to either of us.
William	'tis true but I am at fault, none of it is yours and I will not ever let you condemn yourself for my faults.
Emilia	I know your faults before you know them yourself Will Shakespeare.
William	What are you saying?
Emilia	I also know your strengths, I have been in your audience many times before you were in mine.
William	Then you know my plays?
Emilia	Yes and through your plays I have come to know some of you. Yet, although I was duty bound when I attended, to pretend allegiance to my Lord Chamberlain Hunsden it was you who won my secret devotion.
William	And do you like me?
Emilia	I would say I like you but need we discuss what we can say without speaking?
William	I suppose not, but….
Emilia	No, Will, there is nothing to discuss unless it is poetry. I write too.
William	What have you written?
Emilia	It is called Salve Deus Rex Judaeorum and it is prefaced with warnings about men disposed to evil who though being borne of women do like vipers deface the wombs wherein they were bred.

William	Why so harsh an admonition.
Emilia	You would only ask that because you are a man, do you understand that women are made to suffer needlessly because of the insensitivity and careless lust of men?
William	But for my family, a woman has been the Queen of suffering! Elizabeth has murdered my uncle. You write of hailing the God who is king of the Jews but what of God who is king of the Catholics?
Emilia	I am a Venetian Jew, so am inured to what your family would consider fresh injury, but the domination of women precedes even the persecution of the Jews and long predates this Queens' persecution of Catholics.
William	It is too solemn, let me change the issue? Will you write poetry for me?
Emilia	No, you can write poetry for me and I will write music for you.
William	(Reaching out for her in the bed and cuddling her down under the covers) Well let us work on our first compositions my beautiful Emelia. (they laugh)

(Light fades on the lovers.)

Scene 7.

Enter Jonson

It is 26th September 1598 and an historical event is about to unfold which we discover in this conversation at the Green Dragon.

Exit Jonson

Persons
Richard Burbage
William Shakespeare
Peter Strete (a builder)
John Heminges
Thomas Pope
Augustine Phillips
William Kempe

Wiliam Slye
Nicholas Tooley

Burbage	These negotiations with Giles Alleyn to continue the lease on the Theatre at Blackfriars have become a quagmire and it killed my father last year so I plan to take my revenge on that scavenger; 21 years we have paid his rents and now he says that he will allow only another five years before converting our theatre to some better use.
William	There can be no better use than to have provided a platform for Gentleman of Verona, Comedy of Errors, Love's Labour's Lost, Love's Labour's Won, Midsummer Night's Dream, Merchant of Venice, Richard the Second, Richard the Third, Henry the Fourth, Titus Andronicus and Romeo and Juliet.
Burbage	Agreed William, and your plays shall not lie fallow for want of a theatre so keep writing; let me confide to you and the others what pains I have taken since this scoundrel Alleyn so confounded my father James as to cause his heart to fail. I have noted every plank and nail inserted onto his hallowed turf, the none of which is his, and the whole of which he being an absent landlord he will find has disappeared before he returns. This is why I have called this assembly.
Heminges	What skills have you displayed in addition to the brilliance of your performances?
Burbage	You all knew my Father James, together with myself and brothers, are builders by trade, so that every fitment and improvement is known by me and has been recorded with receipts over these last many years; and more than that, your shares as owners in the Theatre have always been respected in black ink and now can be produced and listed in a Court of law should the need occur.
Phillips	Are you taking us to the Courts Richard, to counter Alleyn's proposal?

Kempe	Surely with the lease expired even the greatest barrister could not demonstrate a bargain which could be enforced?
Burbage	No you are right, the lease has all but expired yet our ownership of every jot and tittle of materials remains with us so long as the same is removed as a tenant's fixture within the effluxion of the leasehold.
William	Are we to lay hands on the plank that is Will's, the nails that are mine, the thatching which belongs to us all in part?
Burbage	Precisely Will, that is precisely it. You might not know it but sitting here with us is London's best builder, allow me to introduce Peter Strete.
Strete	Hello to you all, Rick does me too much a compliment but I can confirm I am a builder and that I have a team of tradesmen at the ready who are second to none.
Phillips	So, what is planned?
Burbage	The Theatre is ours, the land is Alleyn's; we will leave Alleyn his land and we will move the Theatre plank by plank and we will have it done before Alleyn has time to return.
William	How long do you think we have?
Strete	We have quietly surveyed the building and if you examine every plank and bench you will see a builder's mark subtly scrawled upon it so that we know where every piece of the puzzle will fit.
Heminges	And where do we hide our puzzle?
Burbage	It will not be hidden John, it will stand bigger and better on a site I have secured at St. Saviour's Parish near the Rose.
William	And will this withstand the test of law?
Burbage	I have legal opinion that it is more than fair and we have the patronage of the Lord Chamberlain himself to augment the argument.
Phillips	How long before we can tread the boards again?
Burbage	Alleyn will have his tatty piece of land within the week but the new Theatre which we will call the Globe will take all spring to complete.

Strete	I have done all the reckoning and I ask for your patience because what I will build for you will outshine every other theatre in London, you shall have space for one thousand groundlings and more than a thousand in the galleries.
Burbage	Peter's reckoning is that we will have our new playhouse opening in the summer.
Heminges	This is a master stroke Burbage, you are more than the greatest actor and builder but now a magician who can make the end of an era into the coming of a new age, who can pick up a building and march with it across the Thames. Three cheers for Richard Burbage.
All	Hip Hip Hurrah Hip Hip Hurrah Hip Hip Hurrah
William	And three more for Master Strete.
All	Hip Hip Hurrah Hip Hip Hurrah Hip Hip Hurrah
William	And across the stage of this great new Theatre, the Globe, let it be inscribed Totus Mundus Agit Historionem.
Heminges	I agree but what does that mean?
William	All the world's a stage
Phillips	Bravo, and Burbage is the greatest scene changer of them all.
Slye	Or as Alleyn might have it, scene stealer!

Scene 8.

Enter Jonson

Our players, now owners of the most successful of a dozen theatres in London opened their Globe on 12th June 1599 but in early February 1601 the players received a strange request.

Exit Jonson

Persons

Sir Walter Raleigh
Sir Robert Cecil

Enter Raleigh and Cecil

Raleigh	Essex has been on the Queens' business attempting to subdue the Irish rebels under Hugh O'Neill but reports are, that he draws sword only to confer knighthoods on his men.
Cecil	The reports are true, there are more knighthoods in England from Essex than from her Majesty herself!
Raleigh	That sword arm has been busy.
Cecil	And strengthened through such actions to array an army of plotters against her Majesty and he plots with King James of Scotland to take the Crown.
Raleigh	On his return from Ireland he took himself into the Queen's bedchamber thinking he was a favourite who could so announce his return.
Cecil	Our good Privy Council confined him to quarters at York and but for the Queen's tested patience he would have been hanged.
Raleigh	Let us ensure his power is well curbed less his band of many Knights stand with him to challenge the Queen.

Exit Raleigh and Cecil

Scene 9.

Enter Jonson

Essex unbowed by his house arrest attends
with his colleague Lord Meyrick to visit our
players at the Globe.

Persons

Robert Devereux, Second Earl of Essex
Sir Gelly Meyrick
William Shakespeare
Richard Burbage
Augustin Phillips

Meyrick	Mr. Burbage, you know our lord.
Burbage	I am honoured my lord.

79

Essex	The honour is mine Mr. Burbage to make your acquaintance and that of the famous Mr. Shakespeare.
William	Your Lordship my fame is at your disposal.
Essex	I have a special request of the Lord Chamberlain's Men which I believe will find favour with you; if not on account of what the Mountjoy's tell me of your displeasure with our Queen, then, by payment of forty shillings beyond your takings to your company to perform your play Richard the Second.
Phillips	Were we to resurrect that old play my Lord we should have no company to join us it is so old and out of use.
William	My Lord that play has been relegated of late and not without cause.
Essex	That cause I suspect is the scene in Act IV where Bolingbroke utters, "Are you contented to resign the Crown?" for that is the very scene for which I want this performance on Saturday 7th February.
William	Is there a scene that follows on from that which we must perform?
Essex	The less you know the safer you and your fellow players will remain but be assured your play will start the play that follows.
Burbage	This is a risky request Will?
Phillips	We are but humble players reprising an old work and nothing more, and forty shillings is a good night's work.
William	I am for it, but not for the money but my contribution in kind for the injury done to my own.
Meyrick	I think we have general agreement although we have arrived by different ways.
Burbage	I am content to repeat an old play and will leave any new plays for those concerned, for though the bill proclaimed Romeo and Juliet, we'll amend it with the public told our Juliet has taken ill.
William	It is done then my Lords and we shall await upon you for matinee on the seventh.
Essex	Good day to you sirs, we must be on our way.
Burbage	Good day my Lords.

William   Adieu!

Essex and Meyrick leave towards the side of the stage,
        the light darkens on our actors and remains
        on Meyrick and Essex

Essex   You spread the word about the city that
Richard the Second returns to the stage and
on that day I will gather with my Knights to
marry with the audience so emboldened
and take the Crown from this malignant
Queen

Scene 10.

Persons

Enter Jonson

The next day we find our actors
contemplating the merit of their contract
with Essex.

Condell
Burbage
Shakespeare
Phillips

Phillips   (Handling a scroll) I have been summonsed
by the Chief Justice to give deposition of
our little arrangement with Essex, what am
I to say?

Burbage   They know all, and if they don't with Little
Ease at work in the Tower they soon will, so
follow the truth.

William   And what is all the truth

Burbage   Essex with two hundred supporters
marched to take the Crown and was
stopped at Ludgate then fought his way
back to Essex House. He was there besieged
and on threat of his group being burned
alive he did surrender. Now the Queen has
said about our play that she knows she was
Essex's Richard the Second.

Phillips   And thus are we implicated?

William	No we are simply actors who struck a bargain to play to the Earl's fancy unknowing of his ambitions.
Burbage	The Queen will give him no more mercy and says "a senseless ingrate has at last revealed what long has been on his mind."
Phillips	And now I am to be interrogated as though we are part of the conspiracy against her.
William	You are an actor Augustine and now must play your finest part of the dupe who penniless as actors are, was suborned by the offer of forty shillings; tell it all and more as well, there is nothing we can do to save Essex, his day has come and perhaps he knew as much.
Burbage	It would be well if you should out-perform last night's performance as the play seemed to send the crowd to slumber more than revolution.
William	And the spies who loiter everywhere will report as much and that will be to our advantage, so ready yourself Augustine for your most important performance upon which we will all depend.

ACT 7

Enter Jonson

To quote :

"Last scene of all,
  That ends this strange eventful history,
 Is second childishness and mere oblivion,
   Sans teeth, sans eyes, sans taste, sans everything. "

This act does not unfold with scenes as grim as these lines portend but nevertheless rounds upon them as it must for all of us, in the final scene. We move now to the early 1600's when my own star began to shine. William and his players were the Establishment, being known now under the title of the Kings Men. Queen Elizabeth had hanged her last traitor and followed them to the grave to be succeeded by King James. He so endorsed our playwright friend that he took the Lord Chamberlain's company as his own. It was at this time that William's plays began to fade against the brilliance of my own, with plays such as Poetaster, about the great Roman poet Ovid, with boy actors, music and all the new fashion that made Shakespeare's work look dated, or so I thought at the time. William acknowledged my cleverness by performing in my plays Every Man in his Humour and Sejanus.

So here we are and during this Act I will move from the edge of this stage to become a player myself, for William and I became close friends in the last years of his life. The first scene finds us at the Mermaid.

Jonson moves from the side of the stage into centre stage which is set as the Mermaid Tavern.

Spotlight follows Jonson from the side of the stage to the set of the Inn.

Scene 1.

Persons

William Shakespeare
Ben Jonson
Richard Burbage

William	(Enters to find Burbage and Jonson at a table drinking) How are you my good friends?
Burbage	Good day to you Will, you are back from Stratford, how goes it with Anne and the family.
William	Father John is not well but I kept him busy helping me with the purchase of more property and he never ceases to introduce me to his friends as "his famous son" and to remind all and sundry of his coat of arms.
Jonson	Not without right, eh Will?
William	Exactly Ben, not without right?
Burbage	And the others?
William	Well my brothers and sisters are all well, Gilbert, Joan, Richard and Edmund and I have seen to it that Gilbert has some acres to farm.
Jonson	And what of Anne, how is she and how are the girls?

William	Anne is my genius, I want to say that to you both now before I start drinking, she has been my best friend and more besides and of course with her strength the girls are outstanding.
Burbage	You are in good spirits and let me prolong the conversation by buying you some good spirits.
William	Good be upon you Rick Burbage, and tell me of the theatre, what is happening here apart from the tedium of Ben's boy plays.
Jonson	That's enough of that Shakespeare, you are just displaying your jealousy for a superior talent.
William	I won't take your bait Ben but I will give you this compliment, you are a good playwright for a bricklayer!
Jonson	And you Will might remember what Augustus said to Haterius?
William	No Ben, you might remind us.
Jonson	Sufflaminandus erat!
Burbage	Are you insulting our greatest playwright?
Jonson	Not at all, he is an honest man of open and free nature, he has an excellent fancy , brave notions and gentle expressions, whereby he flows with that facility that sometimes it would be better if he stopped ergo sufflaminandus erat, meaning his pipes should be clogged.
Burbage	You jealous swine Jonson, it pains you to give a man credit does it not.
Jonson	No, not at all.
Burbage	If you could write a line as well, you would not need to utter such insults.
Wililam	Careful Richard, those bricklayers hands have strangled a man, poor Gabriel Spencer, and a fellow actor too.
Jonson	What rubbish, that was a fair battle at Hoxton Fields and I survived that free of the law's rebuke.
Burbage	It sounds as though it didn't go so well for Spencer.
Jonson	Alright you've nailed me quite, and I will admit, but only where there is no audience, I love you Will and I would give all I have to have been endowed with your gifts.

William	I take you lightly Ben, you are a good friend and although ready to argument at any time, you are a man who would always leap to my aid and that is something that forgives the rest.
Jonson	Have your drink and let us put our competition to better use and tell me what pours from your pen at the moment.
William	To both of you I can talk without false modesty, we are craftsmen with our words, we all can act, none as well as Richard but we give it our best, and Ben and I are the men of words, it is our passion. We love with them, we fight with them, we arm-wrestle each other with them.
Jonson	And we play our contests to the public who pay us to watch the contest.
William	And so it is, and what a joy to be paid for what we love most.; but I am on a quest to perfect my art before my arm is wracked with cramps and my brain is drying out with old age.
Jonson	Well, tell us what is agitating you?
Wiliam	When the plague closed the theatres I poured myself into the Sonnets and I tried to be true, to be expansive I tried to be fair and kind and true.
Jonson	And what next?
William	Your question my compeer is a great compliment but I will continue. I am completing a rewrite of that old piece called Ur Hamlet, about a Prince of Denmark; there are lots of historical sources but I am plumbing this subject with all my wit to examine the very state of the human mind.
Burbage	Is it a piece I could act?
William	That is the challenge Rick, to deal with the things that I explored in the Sonnets but they are structured pieces and so must this be, but on so much larger a scale.
Jonson	And how are you wrestling with it?
William	That is the whole of it Ben, it is not a wrestle, you know the experience when you are at the threshold, an ale or two and then over you go and the words are flowing?

Jonson	Sometimes I need more than two ales to achieve that mellifluity.
William	Yes but you will be aware of those times when the pen runs with itself and the joy that brings, when eating and sleeping become interruptions?
Jonson	Yes I know that feeling but it is a rare jewel.
William	It is Ben, but when the jewel is before you the exhilaration is immense and it carries you with it and you become in awe of your own creation; it is so parallel to witnessing the birth of your own child.
Burbage	You have me excited Will, what are you calling your play?
William	It needs no more invention than Hamlet, Prince of Denmark.
Jonson	Can you favour us with some of your lines?
William	Let me take you to something that will mean much to us all when Hamlet speaking with actors in the hall at the Castle says, " O it offends me to hear a robustious periwig-pated fellow tear a passion to tatters, to very rags, to split the ears of the groundlings….I could have such a fellow whipped for overdoing Termagant."
Burbage	Bravo, I do most agree.
Jonson	Go on Will, this is good stage direction to all.
William	"Be not too tame either, but let you own discretion be your tutor: suit the action to the word, the word to the action; with this special observance, that thou o'erstep not the modesty of nature: for anything so overdone is from the purpose of playing, whose end, both at the first and now, was and is, to hold as 'twere, the mirror up to nature; to show virtue her own true feature, scorn her own image, and the very age and body of the time his form and pressure." (Act III, Sc. 2)
Jonson	(Taking up his glass) I do more than toast you Will, I bow to you and thank God for your life and your rhymes.
Burbage	I drink to that also Will, god speed your play.

William	And I in return my good friends, (stepping back) look at us, we are pretty things, I do not mean our tatty robes, but our words and deeds and God grant us time to perfect our art before we turn to dust.
Jonson	I'll drink to that!
Burbage	And I again.

Scene 2.

At the Globe Theatre in the Actor's dressing room.

Persons

Burbage
Shakespeare
King James
An Attendant to the King

(Burbage and Shakespeare removing their greasepaint)

Enter the attendant

Attendant	His Highness asks that he might have an audience with you Masters Shakespeare and Burbage.
William	We are honoured, by all means, but is he here?
Attendant	His Highness is coming.
Burbage	We are still covered in the grease and are unwashed.

(Enter King James)

James	Well done Mr. Shakespeare, what a stunning ghost you make, and you Mr. Burbage moved me to the core of my soul.
William	We are most honoured your Majesty but hardly dressed for a King.
James	Your attire matters not, we hastened here on the height of emotion and felt it most right to come at once and the apology is mine.
Burbage	Not at all your Highness, thank you for your compliments.

James	We were moved when it was said of these "Abstracts and brief chronicles of time" that it is "better to have had a bad epitaph than their ill report while you live."
William	Your Highness, what joy it causes to serve a King who honours knowledge.
James	And what joy it gives that King to be patron to such an author, what next subject will your pen favour?
William	I know not what favour this will find your Highness but I am writing of a Moorish patrician married to an English woman.
James	Tell me of this Mr. Shakespeare, it touches on a subject most politic, are you aware of the petitions being made to remit coloured people to their own countries?
William	I am your Highness and I wish to awake some conscience on this subject having among my friends Abdul Ghavid who was the Moorish ambassador to Queen Elizabeth.
James	We are most interested in this story Mr. Shakespeare and it bears the hallmark of a Christian endeavour, but be aware of the Henry Cecil's of London who protest to me about the infiltration of our society by the black man.
William	If I may be permitted to say Your Highness there can often be no offence if the parcel is delivered with courtesy.
James	Indeed that is so Mr. Shakespeare and I wish you well on your endeavour, but should it become a matter of politic I will reserve my position, but I promise you my protection whilesoever you favour our stage with your plays.
William	How can I thank you my Highness?
James	We will be well pleased to see you continue to write and stay with us in good health.
William	Permit me sir, exultant with your visit to commend you with some poetry, " Crowns have their compass, length of days their date, Triumphs their tomb, felicity her fate: Of nought but earth can earth make us partaker, But knowledge makes a King most like his Maker."

James	We are most honoured with that tribute Master Shakespeare and I will remember that all my days.
William	As will I this memorable salutation your Majesty.

The King leaves.

Burbage	How extraordinary a night, and what a triumph, the playing of Hamlet to a full house with the King himself who then comes backstage unannounced as though a fawning groundling!
William	How right you are Richard, and what presence of mind we must have to savour this night as one of the highest points to which we have both ever flown.
Burbage	'Tis true Will, I could not have ever dreamed of this when first I began working with my father as a builder all those years ago in Stratford.
William	Nor I when I set out to Lancashire as a young man to earn my family's keep as a teacher, a wife at home with my parents and two children to feed. What a world this is?
Burbage	And what of your family Will?
Wiliam	They are all growing older as we all are; I have bought the New Place at Stratford, my daughter is soon to marry and I am ready to go back.
Burbage	What to visit again?
William	No Rick, to retire back to the country, you cannot pile laurel upon laurel; I do not boast to have done it all but I have done what I could. I have followed my pen many leagues across the parchment. Perhaps having filled those blank spaces with my ink it is better to go than have to push my pen which till now has let me follow as it drew me on.
Burbage	Why not Will? God bless you, go back to Stratford, manage your estates and visit London when the need drives you.
Wiliam	That is my thinking Rick, none of this is forever and we both have given our most

	when we could. I wish it were otherwise, indeed when I was a young man it little crossed my thoughts that I should not be on this world forever but events have shown me that even the most precious things like my beautiful son Hamnet are only on loan in this place, and I am no different; so my thinking is to leave and enjoy my native country before I am too old to wield an axe or wander in the fields.
Burbage	And what of your plays?
Wililam	That will not cease Richard indeed I have many more planned and I will bring them to London myself and involve myself in the production; however I intend to alter my recurrent attendance upon the stage.
Burbage	And will your parting be a formal affair, I am sure his Highness would make it an occasion of state were you to announce your intent.
Wiliam	No, I will be like the ghost, here, then gone, then here again, so there will be no formal embarkation. I am negotiating to purchase a place in Southwark so that I have a ready place each time I return and little need be known as to whether I am here or Stratford.
Burbage	There's always a new chapter! What a time we've shared Will.
William	And many more to come Rick but there is a right time to remove from centre-stage and with the plague and the continual uncertainty as to whether we can play or not, so by this move I will be relieved of that hurdy-gurdy.

Scene 3.

Enter Jonson

Will began to spend more time back at Stratford but the plays continued and seemed to become more magnificent with every one he wrote.

This scene finds us at Stratford at the New Place in the year 1604.

Exit Jonson

Persons

William
Anne
Mary Shakespeare

(Knocking on the door, William opens it)

William	Mother, how good to see you out and about.
Mary	Oh well Will, it does my aging bones good to walk about and see my son, it is such a wonderful thing to have you back.
Anne	Hello Mary will you have some tea and scones?
Mary	Thank you dear Anne, I would love a cup and the scones smell delicious. What is my oldest boy working on now?
William	I have some land deals that I am pursuing mother and there is always a play to keep me busy.
Mary	What play busies you now son and tell me about King James?
William	Mother you know my actor friends John Heminges, Augustine Phillips and Richard Burbage?
Mary	Yes of course.
William	We are so well favoured that before his coronation James commanded his robe makers, Ede and Ravenscroft to issue us each four and a half yards of scarlet and we all had new doublets and breaches to wear.
Mary	What, the King himself made provision for you all?
William	Aye he did mother, and we attended with all the pomp and ceremony, it was a wonder to behold; there were triumphal

	arches topped with obelisks over the streets for the Kings' entry to London and these towers were seventy feet high!
Mary	And my famous son there to watch!
William	Nay mother not just to watch but I was appointed an attendant upon his Majesty himself.
Anne	Will's company mother, are called the Kings' Men, they are specially appointed as the Kings Players.
Mary	I am so proud of you Will.
William	I am glad you are proud mother but you know this pomp matters little to me.
Mary	It might matter little to you my good son but it means the world to me to see you succeed so and I can tell you it was a great pride to your late father, you made him so happy.
Anne	You are a good man Will Shakespeare, didn't I tell you when you were first courting me that you would be great, I could see it in you.
William	Enough you two, too much, it does me no service to be caught staring at my own reflection.
Anne	Mary there is a universe in his mind that is beyond fathoming.
Mary	You were a kind and loving son Will and so you have proved as a man so be patient enough to hear it from those who love you!
William	Then let me trumpet your praises my dearest wife and mother. What man has there been who has been so favoured with the love you two have selflessly given me. A mother who spent endless hours with me as a child awaking my love of learning and who wept when I had to leave school at fourteen; and then supported me when I came to her with news of my pregnant lover; who then loved you Anne as though you were her own daughter; and then you dear Anne a more devoted friend and wife no man ever had. You were there for me when full of the fears of youth, without prospects or a trade you took me in to your heart and loved me and have never once

	ceased to support me. You have waited patiently upon me while I chased the phantom fame.
Anne	It is for the love you helped me find within myself that I have given what I have and there has been no cost to me Will.
Mary	All these circles are complete Will, we have each other, one another, and we are happy and well and we are glad to know it!
William	Indeed we are mother indeed we are, now both of you give me your arms so that we can embrace.

(They embrace one another in a circle)

Mary	Will you be here this Christmas Will?
William	I go back to London with a play about a Scottish King like our good King James but after that is performed we have to ready the company for the Christmas revels at Hampton Court.
Anne	It is a very busy time for Will, mother, while the Court feasts and enjoy the revels, Will and Rick and the company have 38 plays that will be acted over the two weeks.
Mary	One Christmas you must deny the King and be back here with us all Will, promise me that won't you?
William	I do promise mother, not this year though, with the King new installed we must cement our company's place and the rewards will see me well set for retirement.
Mary	It is such a busy round for you Will.
William	It is not too much mother; and with the success of it all I have withdrawn from acting and have more time to write. This last year the company performed 150 times, almost twice a week but the Christmas revels are very demanding although it is a joy to boot.
Mary	And what plays will you do for his Highness.
William	Measure for Measure on Boxing Day, then Love's Labours Lost and many many others, but we are professionals mother, and we can do them blindfold if we must.

Anne	And tonight mother we are guests of the Halls, you know their young son the physician is quite enamoured of our Susanna.
Mary	She is a beautiful girl my grand-daughter, so he had better be a good man.
William	He is a good man mother, you can trust Susanna's mind on that.
Anne	Let's have our tea and scones then and enjoy this happy day.

Scene 4.

Enter Jonson

It is November 1605 and our playwright is in London at the Globe theatre assisting in the production of Macbeth.

Persons

Burbage
William
Judith Shakespeare

(Enter Judith to backstage where she finds her father and Richard Burbage looking at scripts)

William	Judith, how does the day find you?
Judith	Father the whole of London is abuzz.
Burbage	Hello Judith, London is always abuzz and never stops to amaze us country folk!
Judith	It is more than that Richard, the criers say there has been plot to blow up the politicians and the Royal Family at Westminster.
William	You are playing with us Judy?
Judith	No father, it is true, I will not joke about what I have heard.
William	'Zounds, then the predictions of the astrologers of doom have materialized.
Burbage	We've had eclipses and strange weather and now this!
Judith	In the street they are saying barrels of gunpowder were found under Parliament,

	tons of it, enough to blow them all to Democritus' attomes.
William	There is little peace in politics and now the dogs will be baying for papists under every cobble and kerb.
Burbage	We have seen it all before and the Puritans will want the theatres closed yet again.
William	And as we've seen it, so it shall be, the people will not take kindly to losing their theatre so let us just keep a cool vigil on the whole cycle as it unfolds.
Burbage	They'll roll out the old cart about you being a papist poet Will.
William	Of course they will but it all passes, and this time they will tie my family into it because Judith has been summonsed for not attending Protestant Easter Communion, I brought her down with me from Stratford to see what could be done.
Judith	And now this Father, I will be roped in as a papist.
William	No I'll see to it that it passes over you Judith, don't fear that; you have just joined a long line of Shakespeare dissenters, your grandfather had to spend some days in the Tower but I will have it fixed so that your summons is assuaged.
Burbage	There are always the barrow pushers who come out at these times.
William	But we Richard have the most powerful barrow of them all with the theatre and I mean to do some pushing myself. I have been working on a play with some other playwrights about Thomas More but we are negotiating its release with the Stationers Company.
Burbage	Aye, the King's censors.
William	That they are Rick, but it is a skill to slip the message past them. This time they are more alert and although they accept the attack of the mob against the immigrant asylum seekers they are not so keen on the Christian remonstration of Sir Thomas against the mob when he abjures them to "look into their hearts at their monstrous inhumanity."

Judith	One would think they would welcome the true Christian virtue.
William	Oh no, these are they who police our thinking, which is ironic given how little knowledge of thinking they possess; however if they see fit to ban this work of history I will get the message through to King James with King Lear whom I lead through my play, to seeing the error of his ways.
Judith	Yes but the King proclaims the royal line as gods on earth for whom no-one can make a challenge.
William	That is the beauty of the history play, for it is not an affront to our godly King to regale him with a knowledge of history; if in the hearing it should awaken his conscience then that is an accident of the telling.
Burbage	A well executed accident if I know you Will.
William	That might be so Richard but I am an unrepentant offender and I have another play in the wings, more history, quite ancient.
Burbage	And what is this?
William	It is the history of Coriolanus, which I have exhumed from Plutarch's Lives.
Burbage	And dare I ask is this pure history Will?
William	Oh yes, pure history leavened with a little contemporaniety of the Diggers of Warwickshire who will appear in my play, dressed in ancient attire, and will not at first be recognized and when they are, the justice of their claims will be evident.
Judith	I fear for these poor diggers, all they want is that the common fields not be closed to them.
Burbage	The mood of the time can be guessed from this Royal line's history I fear; whatever the right of the Diggers' claims, if their challenge be too strong they will be crushed.
William	Let us pray that can be avoided.
Burbage	Have you told Judith of our new playhouse Will?
Judith	Father told me that you are opening a winter playhouse at Blackfriars.

Burbage	Indeed we are, it is a promising venture; it is a smaller theatre than the Globe but not exposed to the elements, but the casements can be opened to bring in the daylight during matinees.
William	And we have our new play Cardenio which follows the story of Don Quixote and will be played in the new style with boy singers, soft light and Italian lute music.
Burbage	Do you know Judith, we are going to be right nearby the Mermaid and for the occasion some of us are having our portraits painted so that they might be hanged in the foyer.
William	You should be careful Richard for if you identify yourself too closely with my plays with your face displayed so you might indeed find yourself hanged in the foyer.

Scene 5.

Enter Jonson

	Our players did launch their new indoor theatre at Blackfriars and it was a resounding success. In 1610 we find William with his colleagues at the Mermaid celebrating their latest triumph.

Exit Jonson

Persons

Richard Burbage
Laurence Fletcher
William Shakespeare
John Heminges
Henry Condell
Captain Newport

(All seated at a table in the Mermaid Tavern)

Burbage	Gentleman I propose a toast to our latest triumph with Pericles the Prince of Tyre

	filling our coffers and our debts all paid on Blackfriars.
Heminges	What a boon it has been to do our summer season at the Globe and then have Blackfriars for the winter.
William	But let us toast the memory of our beloved friend and actor Will Sly whose share of the bounty needs go to his kin.
All	To Will Sly
Burbage	May God have mercy on his soul.
William	Amen.
Fletcher	While dwelling on the lugubrious, let me remind you that the challenge to our playing on the north bank still persists.
Condell	The Lord Mayor has never accepted our little theatre in Blackfriars, but he has been proven powerless to move us because the land is the Crown's not the property of the City Corporations.
Fletcher	Indeed, and after the King expressed his gratitude personally to our esteemed playwright William for the compliment paid to his majesty in Macbeth, our position seemed inviolable; but now the Corporation takes a different tack and seeks to buy our theatre and rent it back.
William	There might be little threat in that if the amount offered is sufficiently grand.
Fletcher	The offer is for six thousand one hundred and sixty six pounds, thirteen shillings and four pence, with each of us to be paid according to his share plus emoluments for the hired men and the widows and orphans of our deceased members making a total of over seven thousand pounds!
Heminges	That is well worth the consideration!
William	So long as we can continue to stage our plays it matters not to me if we should in the meantime be enriched by this proposal.
Fletcher	I am of the same mind, what do the rest of the sharers say?
Heminges	I am agreed
Condell	As are we all.
Burbage	(Aside to William) Will, now that the business of the sharers is done, come with me over to meet Captain Newport who has

	a story to tell which might well found another play.
William	Who is this fellow Rick?
Burbage	I know you are always looking for a good yarn Will and Captain Newport has just returned from the area they call the Western Indies and he is about to go to book.
William	Very well Rick, lead me on.

(They approach Captain Newport sitting drinking)

Burbage	Captain Newport.
Newport	Oh Burbage, how are you?
Burbage	Never been better Captain. Allow me to introduce my colleague Will Shakespeare.
Newport	What a pleasure to meet you sir, our famous playwright.
William	Thankyou very much Captain Newport.
Burbage	Captain, I have been telling Will about your book and I was hopeful that you would share some of its tales with Will who is looking for material for a new play.
Newport	Oh, that would be too great an Honour, but if you are interested Will, then I can tell you some of my story.
William	Indeed Captain Newport I am very interested.
Newport	I have handed over my logs to Sir Thomas Gates and Sir George Somers concerning my explorations in the West Indies, do you know where that is, Will?
William	Off the American coast is it not?
Newport	Well roundabouts there, yes it is. Our tale goes back to 24th July 1609 when I captained the ship Sea Adventure for the Virginia Company. We had set out on 2nd June from Plymouth bound for Virginia and although I captained the ship it was the flagship of the fleet. The fleet was under the command of Admiral Sir George Somers because we were conveying the new governor of Virginia Sir Thomas Gates to America.
William	Oh you were part of the famous shipwreck?
Newport	That was us, sir, indeed it was; well, as I said it all changed on 24th July 1609 for then

	a wild storm broke up our fleet and we were separated and fight though we did, our great ship was lost.
William	Did you lose men?
Newport	Nary a one, Mr. Shakespeare; we all boarded the lifeboats and made way towards the island of Bermuda once the sea had calmed; now there was some good trepidation among us because of the reputation passed on from the sailors that this was a land of barbarians.
William	Have you read Florio's translation of Montaigne's book on the Caribbeans?
Newport	Aye, I have, and what direct knowledge he had I do not know, but his writing on the subject is not far from the truth. Instead of having to protect ourselves we were treated most kindly by these native peoples.
William	And Captain Newport, my interest aroused, can you provide me with the proofs of your new book?
Newport	It would be my honour to do so Mr. Shakespeare and should you need to refer to it in any play you might wish to write, you may do so as my guest, without need for attribution. I do ask that you pay proper respect however to the gentle nature of these good folk.
William	You have my word on that, but tell us the end of your tale.
Newport	Well, frankly I was in no hurry to leave that place. I found the life so congenial, as Montaigne idealized, so it was, no "politic superiority; no use of service, of riches or of poverty.." In truth it would not have mattered had we remained for the rest of the fleet made it to Jamestown and after a respectable time presumed us all lost in the storm. In the midst of this paradise I was in the company of men who had no rank in such a place, and it agitated them, Sir George to be governing and Sir Thomas to be admiralling so under their direction mustering as little haste as I could disguise as vigour, we reassembled our small boats and rigging and set off in search of

Jamestown. Nine months later on 23rd May 1610 our two boats landed at Jamestown. We had not lost a man, we had the full complement and the people of Jamestown were so astonished at first they thought we were ghosts. In truth gentlemen, there was more risk of loss of men to the delights of the Caribbean than to any storm that ravaged us; but there was little choice, so I had hunted my men up from where'er they were and presented them to the Admiral for our sad departure.

William	A conflict between duty and happiness.
Newport	It is the rule of life is it not.
William	(Stands with Burbage to take his leave) You might well be right, sir. I look forward to receiving your book and in return when a play emerges, you shall have a true copy and be invited to the best box in our theatre.
Newport	Thank you sir, and it will be my honour to attend.
Burbage	Good day to you Captain Newport and I am most obliged for sharing that with me and Will.
Newport	Richard, you are welcome any time, god speed you both.

Burbage and Shakespeare exit. Scene Ends.

Scene 6.

Enter Jonson

Our great playwright is now 48 and spending most of his time at Stratford with Anne. We find him at his home, called the New Place in the kitchen with his quill and papers.

Persons

William
Anne
Richard Burbage

Anne	It is good to have our quiet times together Will, I trust it doesn't irk you, after the business of London.
Will	Not at all Anne, I am in raptures to be back in Stratford with my kin, though so much has been lost or changed; my parents now both gone, Susanna married to a Protestant doctor!
Anne	It is still a family home Will, with Susanna and John and our beautiful granddaughter Elizabeth, Judith as well.
William	I am not mournful but I have lost my brothers Edmund, Richard and now Gilbert and it hurts me deeply in that dark place in my heart where Hamnet lies.
Anne	Even you Will, with your mind that extends throughout the universe, do not have an answer for death any more than I and so our way is simply to grieve it and then return to what life remains.
William	'Tis true Anne, but its mystery is a fertile source for imagination and fear.
Anne	Life continues Will and we must cherish every day, think on the young ones that have come, and your sister Joan and your nephews and nieces, William, Mary, Thomas and Michael.
William	I could scarcely have imagined the events of our lives Anne, but I tell you again that I love you and you have so many times saved my life, for my mind when idle turns inward and consumes me, and so it is always with your encouragement I take up the quill and rise above that inward consumption with the words that spring forth.
Anne	Let me promote that feeling again Will, it must be time to take up the quill, is there a theme floating in space.
William	I have been blessed with good sleep back here in Stratford and my dreams take me to a place where the ideas come and I keep returning to the Caribbean islands.
Anne	And where are they?
William	In the Western Indies off the coast of America. I have been given a tale of a

shipwreck by a captain I met in London and it churns away inside me; I want to write this one consummation where I conclude my inner thoughts which I have hitherto buried deep inside my Sonnets.

Anne   And tell me the tale in which you will wrap your truths Will?

William   I have my Prince of Milan, Prospero I call him. He is a past prince, in that although being in line for power, dedicates himself to study of the secret arts; and, being so distracted it creates a scene where his brother Antonio takes opportunity to make a pact with the King of Naples to take Prospero's power and banish him with his daughter Miranda.

Anne   And how is this banishment achieved?

William   Antonio's henchmen abandon Prospero and his daughter Miranda to the sea in a small bark, but the loyal servant Gonzalo ensures that they have provision to live should they survive the sea.

Anne   Do they survive this ordeal?

William   They do, and the magical powers of Prospero continue to grow for he has with him his books and his charms, the very same skills that enable him to provide his young daughter Miranda with her education.

Anne   How do you unfold this evil course of events?

William   Prospero by his powers, we know not what; whether in compelling events or merely foreseeing them, brings his enemies to the shore of the very island where he himself has lived in exile.

Anne   How did that come to pass?

William   Again a violent sea, in a an ocean renowned for it, and then a shipwreck delivering the same Antonio onto those shores with Ferdinand, the son of his arch enemy, the King of Naples and their retainers including the ever loyal Gonzalo, and so our plot is laid.

Anne   Continue Will, I am following this tale.

William	It is then revealed to my audience that Prospero has indeed a spirit in his service, a spirit called Ariel who to its master's command has indeed summonsed the wind that brought the enemy to Prospero's isle.
Anne	And how did Prospero obtain the service of such a powerful spirit as Ariel?
William	One thing connects to another; Ariel was caught under the spell of an evil witching hag I call Sycorax and it is my protagonist Prospero who has freed Ariel from the grip of Sycorax.
Anne	But in return Ariel is enslaved by Prospero?
William	As always Anne you leap ahead of me, but let the play unfold.
Anne	I am sorry Will, go on.
William	Sycorax herself had been banished to this very isle for her mischief and sorcery but was with child when left abandoned by sailors, and this Ariel was her servant. The hag duly gave birth to a "freckled whelp, hag-born, not honoured with a human shape" and then in anger with Ariel's refusal to perform some evil act, did put a spell upon her, unable to be reversed.
Anne	And then?
William	And then , Sycorax dies and Prospero coming upon this wailing sound discovers the spirit of Ariel trapped inside a cloven pine and with his magical powers frees Ariel but as you say, freed into the service of Prospero, who also takes the hag's child, Caliban into his service.
Anne	What purpose do you weave with the majesty of your words Will?
William	It is this and nothing more Anne, to wrestle with Christ's abjuration in the Sermon on the Mount to love thine enemies. What sense can I make of that or have I made of that in this life of mine where for good reason I would at times, had I the power, have cast my enemies down with more than a thousand blows, for that is how it was meted out to those I loved.
Anne	There is a higher wisdom in Christ's words, is there not?

William	I come to that in the last Act, here is a man possessed by learning of the power to manipulate, not just trapped spirits and other people but the very world and its climate, a man at the height of powers but at what price? He has lived with his hate these years and with it the power to control and aye destroy has multiplied, and then love intervenes to put his beloved daughter in love with the son of his hated enemy the King of Naples.
Anne	It is a superb consummation Will, how do you unfold this epiphany?
William	With these words from Prospero after a mere spirit of the air reminds him of what it is to be human in the truest sense, we have Prospero, saying "Hast thou, which art but air, a touch, a feeling of their afflictions? And shall not myself, One of their kind, that relish all as sharply, Passion as they, be kindlier than thou art? Though with their high wrongs I am struck to the quick, Yet, with my nobler reason, 'gainst my fury Do I take part; the rarer action is in virtue than in vengeance."
Anne	That is the teaching Will, but not just with reason is that made, surely in faith.
William	For me Anne there can be no faith until I have reasoned it out and my reason is that hate infects the hater and imprisons him, banishes him to a cell, to an island of his own thought.
Anne	How beautifully you craft your words Will, I love that you share these things with me.
William	Can I ever tell you Anne, that you were the first to believe in me, can you ever imagine how I may have been muted if someone had discouraged me, when I was a fragile boy, or how I could have stumbled when discouraged by others if you had not helped me believe, I am forever grateful.
Anne	Let me accept your gratitude on condition you accept mine for the joy you have given me, the children and the comfort and most of all the universe you have shown me outside the world of Shottery.

William	Whilst the talk is so intense Anne, let me raise another matter lest I should go before you;
Anne	Must we talk of this?
William	Aye we must, there is much to consider. We have considerable property both here and in London and my shares in the theatres. Like Prospero, I have had to embrace a son in law of a different faith, John, though a Protestant is a good man and has agreed to be my executor. If the property descends to you, then by law your male in-laws might upon your death lay a stronger hand than our own daughters upon it; so it is written in the will that apart from some trifles all assets go to Judith and Susanna. I have John Hall's solemn word, and you need it not from the girls, that you will be cared for till the day you die, should I predecease you. The bed, which was willed us by your father is the only specific bequest to you, but that is not in spite, it is for the curious reasons of the law, do you agree.
Anne	Of course I agree, and then if brothers of mine want my estate, then they shall inherit the bed, an ornament anyway, too hard for sleeping except for overstaying guests, and the rest will go to the girls, that is what I would want….
William	That said then, should I take ill, please ensure my will is signed and witnessed as amended so to read, for I am too busy with my play the Tempest at this time to see the attorney.
Anne	You have my solemn promise, but I pray that it will not happen in this way; don't wish it upon yourself, having had the longer visit so far to this earth, I consider it more meet that I should be first to leave, so this, I trust is an idle argument.

Scene 7.

Enter Jonson

In most ways I regret my part in this scene and yet it is written into history and is true that this night we three were at Stratford at the Inn and it is, 22nd April 1616, the day before William's birthday.

Persons
William
Michael Drayton
Ben Jonson
John Hall
Susanna Shakespeare
A Priest

(The three writers are drinking at the Inn)

Jonson	You are not as versed as I in the art of imbibing Will, and yet tonight you are putting me to shame.
Drayton	You do look ill Will, it might be time to rest the beer upon the table.
William	I am tired from my travels to and from London to deal with the rebuilding of the Globe. It has been a good year, dear Judith has married the vintner, Thomas Quiney and we have it in train to rebuild the Globe better than before.
Drayton	Is it the simple truth that the cannon firing in Henry VIII set the thatch alight?
William	(coughing and leaning for breath on the table) It is as simple as that Michael, but the blessing is that only one man was injured and he was a drunken groundling too slow in leaving, but the added blessing was that his drinking companions had enough beer remaining to douse his flaming breeches. (laughing but doubling up with it all)
Jonson	Are you alright Will?
William	I feel very poor Ben and it is not the beer, I have trouble taking breath. (He falls to the table)
Jonson	(Leaps from his seat and goes to William) My God, Will are you alright.
William	Oh, I am reeling Ben, and I have a fever that has come upon me, I have a foreboding so never mind the law! Give me your word

	that you will find a priest of the old faith to attend me.
Drayton	Is it come to that?
Jonson	I pray not, but he seems grave, Michael run to the New Place and waken John Hall, go with all speed.

(William slumps back face upon is hands at the table)

Enter in great haste Dr. John Hall, Susanna and Drayton.

Susanna	(rushing to her father and trying to rouse him but he only murmurs) Father, oh dear God don't take him from us, please, please (becoming hysterical)
Hall	Ben take Susanna aside and Michael help me lay him out and bring a blanket.

(They lay the Bard out on the ground, he is grey and breathing faintly)

Can you hear me Will (takes his pulse, loosens his collar, then puts his ear to his chest)

Jonson	(Leaving Susanna weeping on a chair to the left of stage in half darkness, a soft light suffuses the grey face of our Bard) What is it John, can it be mended?
Hall	I fear not Ben, there is little pulse and great irregularity in the heart, we should lift him gently and take him to his home.
Jonson	(Joining them in the lifting and carrying him from the stage, Susanna following lamely behind clutching her long night-dress to her mouth to suppress the sobbing) Do not think I am abandoning him, but once at home I do one last thing for my beloved friend.

(In the bedroom of the New Place, the Bard lies peacefully as a priest delivers the Last Rites,

Anne by his side clutching his hand,
Susanna, Dr. Hall, Drayton and Jonson look
on sadly.)

Priest   (Annointing William with oil across the
            eyes, ears, mouth and hands, slowly)
            Through this holy unction and His own
            most tender mercy may the Lord pardon
            thee whatever sins or faults thou hast
            committed by sight, by hearing, smell, taste,
            touch, in the name of the Father, and the
            Son and the Holy Spirit, Amen.

The light on the stage slowly fades as each actor remains
            transfixed into the Darkness.

                    END.

                    Notes

Notes

Notes

Made in the USA
Columbia, SC
14 October 2018